LANGUAGES AND LINGUISTICS

USING ALTERNATIVE ASSESSMENT TO IMPROVE EFL LEARNERS' LEARNING ACHIEVEMENT

FROM THEORY TO PRACTICE

T0401305

LANGUAGES AND LINGUISTICS

Additional books and e-books in this series can be found on Nova's website under the Series tab.

EDUCATION IN A COMPETITIVE AND GLOBALIZING WORLD

Additional books and e-books in this series can be found on Nova's website under the Series tab.

LANGUAGES AND LINGUISTICS

USING ALTERNATIVE ASSESSMENT TO IMPROVE EFL LEARNERS' LEARNING ACHIEVEMENT

FROM THEORY TO PRACTICE

HOANG YEN PHUONG

AND

THI VAN SU NGUYEN

EDITORS

nova
science publishers
New York

NOTICE TO THE READER

The Publisher has taken reasonable care in the preparation of this book, but makes no expressed or implied warranty of any kind and assumes no responsibility for any errors or omissions. No liability is assumed for incidental or consequential damages in connection with or arising out of information contained in this book. The Publisher shall not be liable for any special, consequential, or exemplary damages resulting, in whole or in part, from the readers' use of, or reliance upon, this material. Any parts of this book based on government reports are so indicated and copyright is claimed for those parts to the extent applicable to compilations of such works.

Independent verification should be sought for any data, advice or recommendations contained in this book. In addition, no responsibility is assumed by the Publisher for any injury and/or damage to persons or property arising from any methods, products, instructions, ideas or otherwise contained in this publication.

This publication is designed to provide accurate and authoritative information with regard to the subject matter covered herein. It is sold with the clear understanding that the Publisher is not engaged in rendering legal or any other professional services. If legal or any other expert assistance is required, the services of a competent person should be sought. FROM A DECLARATION OF PARTICIPANTS JOINTLY ADOPTED BY A COMMITTEE OF THE AMERICAN BAR ASSOCIATION AND A COMMITTEE OF PUBLISHERS.

Additional color graphics may be available in the e-book version of this book.

Library of Congress Cataloging-in-Publication Data

ISBN: 978-1-53615-161-9

Published by Nova Science Publishers, Inc. † *New York*

CONTENTS

Contents

PREFACE

This book reviews recent theory and research on language alternative assessment in EFL (English as a Foreign Language) classroom contexts and offers pedagogical implications for foreign/second language practitioners, administrators and presents future research directions for language researchers.

Language testing has been extensively reviewed and researched in the past decades (Bachman & Palmer, 1996; Brown, 1995; Carr, 2011). Language teachers often have to develop their tests, based upon test techniques or strategies suggested from popular testing textbooks. However, it is commonly known that that such tests do not provide EFL contexts with useful washback effects. Alternative assessment approaches (portfolios, journals, self-assessment, peer-assessment, classroom observations, conferences and interviews) offer a solution with great potential. First and foremost, alternative assessment approaches help measure students' ability to use English holistically in real-life situations (Bailey, 1998) since most forms of alternative assessment replicate real-world communication and situations. Second, alternative assessment approaches can offer a comprehensive and accurate picture of students' overall competence in English because they have to be conducted over a period of time, rather than giving teachers a snapshot of students' achievement at a particular point in time through the use of final exams (Dickli, 2003). Third, alternative assessment approaches are student-centered, so they offer students a sense of control over their own learning (Richards & Renandya, 2002). With alternative methods of assessment, students can demonstrate what they have actually learnt and how well they can use what they have learnt (OppBeckman & Klinghammer, 2006). Last but not least, alternative assessment provides information on the strengths and weaknesses of each individual student (Huerta-Macías, 2002), which will direct the teacher and student to specific areas where the student needs advice for improvement.

Recently, the testing and assessment agenda has shifted its attention to formative assessment, a recognition that alternative assessment approaches have huge potential in teaching practices. A few countries have restructured their language curriculum allowing teachers more agency in the process of designing assessment types and activities, alternative assessment included. However, alternative assessment has rarely been systematically reviewed and addressed in those reformed contexts. Here and there, alternative assessment is revisited and ideas for its implications in the language curriculum are suggested (Al-Mahrooqi, 2018; Al Ruqueishi, 2015; Dickli, 2003; Worley, 2001). Attempts to review theoretical framework of alternative assessment in a variety of EFL contexts, for each individual sub-skill are therefore needed if a solid theoretical background on alternative assessment in EFL teaching and learning is to be established. While reviews of alternative assessment approaches are scarce, empirical studies on the benefits and limitations of those alternative assessment strategies and techniques for language learning tend to be even more limited. Although Brown and Hudson (1998) argue for the acceptance of alternative assessment in language teaching and learning, they also warned that there might be issues related to reliability, validity and time consumption, especially if different forms of alternative assessment are not tried and supported by research. Language teaching professionals are also becoming increasingly aware of the role of some alternatives to traditional assessment practices, but scientific evidence is needed to validate its effectiveness, to decrease the negative aspects, and to inform administrators and curriculum developers about the current theory and practices of alternative in diverse contexts. Additional empirical research is needed to validate the effectiveness of alternative assessment strategies, both at an individual class or classroom level, and on a broader scale across different age groups, learning levels and educational institutions.

Therefore, this book is an effort to review the theoretical framework for the use of alternative assessment in EFL contexts and at the same time, provides a collection of empirical research on alternative assessment for different groups of EFL learners in various classroom contexts. The aim of the book is not just to simply review the past literature on alternative assessment in EFL contexts. Rather it aims to evaluate current language policy reforms in which opportunities for alternative assessment are incorporated, and recent developments and possibilities for alternative assessment implementation in specific language skills are encouraged. The book thus provides empirical findings specific to certain sub-skills using alternative assessment strategies in EFL contexts, the majority of which takes place in Vietnam. Both the theoretical framework, and the insights and implications from the empirical research described in the book will make alternative assessment more accessible to language teachers in the most relevant and practical way.

The Intended Audience of the Book

This book is intended for those who are interested in language teaching and assessment in EFL contexts. It is particularly directed at language practitioners and teacher trainers who wish to explore the different ways in which assessment can be implemented formatively, rather than conventional language testing techniques. Because the book explores recent developments in approaches to language assessment, it will appeal to students in second and foreign language courses and to researchers in the field of language teaching and assessment. It is also helpful for language policy makers and curriculum designers with regards to curriculum reform and syllabus design.

The Organization of the Book

The book consists of eight chapters organized into two parts. Part I (chapters 1-4) reviews theories of alternative assessment at policy level and classroom level, targeting at specific language skills, whereas Part II (chapters 5-7) provides empirical research findings related to theories reviewed in the first part.

Chapter 1, entitled **"The use of alternative assessment in language teaching context: A review of portfolio assessment in L2/EFL writing courses"** presents the theoretical basis of alternative or formative assessment and focuses on one type of alternative assessment: portfolio assessment in writing skill. The review clarifies why portfolio assessment might lead to enhanced learning with affective and metacognitive benefits. Issues hinder successful portfolio implementation in L2 and EFL writing courses are discussed and debated. Implications for pedagogical practices and research are suggested.

Chapter 2, entitled **"English Curriculum Reform and Formative Assessment Policies: Cross-case analysis -Implications for Alternative Assessment Research in Vietnam"** reviews the advantages of alternative assessment and the opportunities for its implementation in the contexts of language curriculum reforms. Two reformed language curricula and assessment policies: Chinese College English Reforms and Vietnamese General English Reforms are examined and implications for future research related to alternative types of language assessments are presented.

Chapter 3, **"The use of self-assessment to improve EFL students' speaking performance: A review",** on the other hand, provides a thematic review on the benefits of self-assessment in speaking skill. The review demonstrates (1) contradictory ideas on the use of self-assessment analyses (2) studies on the effects of self-assessment on students' speaking skills in the English as a foreign language context (EFL). Pedagogical implications and recommendations related to self-assessment are suggested.

Chapter 4, **"Performance-based assessment: Implications to English language classrooms",** discusses performance-based assessment as an alternative assessment. The chapter outlines key aspects of performance-based assessment: its underpinning philosophies, characteristics, and positive and negative washback effects. The implications of assessments based on students' performance in English language classrooms are discussed.

Chapter 5, **"Impact of Online Peer Feedback on Students' Writing Performance and Attitude"** investigates whether peer feedback on one type of social media can help students improve their writing performance in high school contexts. The chapter reports finding of an experimental study, using a one-group design. Some significant challenging problems students faced when giving feedback online were highlighted and compared in light of past research on using peer feedback as a form of alternative assessment.

Chapter 6, **"Benefits and Challenges of Using Analytic Rubrics for Students' Speaking Self-Assessment Rubric"**, relates to Chapter 3, Performance-Based Assessment and using rubric as one way to optimize students' performances. The results reveal various benefits and problems of using analytic rubrics for students' self-assessment of speaking skills from students' perspectives, which will be of interest to language teachers.

Chapter 7, **"The Implementation of Portfolios in Academic Writing Classroom"** is linked to Chapter 1 by empirically addressing how portfolios develop students' autonomy in an academic writing class. The analysis of the collected data shows that the portfolio assessment helps students develop their responsibility, motivation, and self-confidence which contribute to the willingness to work independently of autonomous learners. Differences between the implementation and the effectiveness of the paper-based portfolio and E-portfolio groups were found and discussed.

As the chapters describe, the current book reviews widely used alternative assessment strategies, their advantages and disadvantages for assessing specific language skills, and their potential use in the current English reformed curriculum for secondary and college or university students. It examines a number of alternative assessment uses in Vietnamese contexts where the use of alternative assessment is encouraged to supplement the conventional paper and pencil testing system. New insights, both theoretical and empirical, emerging from this book help fill some current gaps in the language alternative assessment discourse.

All the contributors to this book firmly believe that alternative approaches for assessing English language skills in and outside the classroom, described in this book or elsewhere in the literature, provide a great many benefits over more conventional pen and paper end-of-course examinations. We hope that the theoretical foundations and empirical research described here will encourage teachers and those who are involved in educational policy and curriculum development to trial, adapt and implement alternative approaches in English language teaching and assessment. We also wish to stress the need for further empirical research to evaluate different assessment strategies for each language skill, and to compare their benefits and drawbacks from the perspective of both students and teachers. Wider adoption of these approaches and further empirical research on their use is likely to have a significant positive impact on learning outcomes for EFL students in Vietnam and elsewhere.

Hoang Yen Phuong, PhD
Thi Van Su Nguyen, PhD

In: Using Alternative Assessment …   ISBN: 978-1-53615-161-9
Editors: Hoang Yen Phuong et al.   © 2019 Nova Science Publishers, Inc.

Chapter 1

THE USE OF ALTERNATIVE ASSESSMENT IN LANGUAGE TEACHING CONTEXT: A REVIEW OF PORTFOLIO ASSESSMENT IN L2/EFL WRITING COURSES

Anh Nguyet Diep[1,*], Chang Zhu[1]
and Minh Hien Vo[1,2]
Department of Educational Sciences,
Vrije Universiteit Brussel, Brussels, Belgium
Graduate School, Can Tho University, Can Tho, Vietnam

ABSTRACT

To support students' learning, new approaches to assessment are implemented next to innovative methods of English as a second language (L2) or foreign language teaching (EFL). Alternative forms of assessment of a formative rather than a summative nature are increasingly endorsed by language teaching faculty. Among these, there has been a growing trend in the use of portfolio assessment. Nevertheless, as portfolio assessment has

* Corresponding Author's E-mail: diep.anh.nguyet@vub.be.

been mainly implemented in other fields such as visual arts, health, and architecture, its relevance, reliability, and validity in L2 and EFL are still topics worth researching. The aim of this book chapter is to review the theoretical basis of alternative or formative assessment and the implementation of one of its types, namely portfolio assessment in L2 and EFL contexts. A thematic literature review was conducted based on the predetermined research objectives. The findings revealed that portfolio assessment has resulted in enhanced learning accompanied by affective and metacognitive benefits. However, issues related to the reliability of assessment criteria, students' treatment and provision of feedback, and students' reflection and capacity in compiling portfolios are still factors that hinder successful portfolio implementation in L2 and EFL writing courses. Based on the findings, implications for pedagogical practices and research are put forward.

Keywords: alternative/formative assessment, portfolio assessment, second/foreign language teaching and assessment

INTRODUCTION

Assessment is a continuous process, the primary purpose of which is to improve student learning (Gronlund, 2006). It is generally acknowledged that assessment has a deep influence on what and how much students learn and how effectively they learn, and the quality of assessment is a key feature of successful teaching (Shihab, 2011). According to William and Black (1996), assessment can be viewed as a cycle of three phases: eliciting evidence, interpreting evidence and taking actions. Teachers are supposed to have a clear and complete comprehension of the learning objectives, have the insight to see whether these goals are being met, and finally, have strong ability to analyze and interpret the evidence gathered from the result of assessment when designing classroom assessment. A good assessment task should ask students for evidence of their learning and the knowledge they have mastered.

When teachers are designing and implementing an assessment, there are several points teachers should bear in mind. Firstly, assessment needs to be "fit-for-purpose," that is, it should enable the evaluation of the extent to which learners have learned and the extent to which they can demonstrate that learning (Brown & Smith, 1997). Educators need to think not only about what they are testing and how they are testing, but also why they are testing particular study points. Secondly, what types of assessment instruments they can use should fit their aims of testing. Teachers should choose methods which are in accordance with the assessment context or environment. There are two main assessment methods: Formative assessment and Summative assessment. According to William and Black (1996), summative assessment tests are designed to judge the extent of students' learning of the material for the purpose of grading, certification, etc. and formative assessment tests are designed to help students to improve what they wish to do.

In the field of EFL and L2 teaching, not taking into account the high-stake tests employed to differentiate students' language competence, alternative forms of assessment, including performance-based, informal assessment, or authentic assessment (Anderson, 1998), are gaining attention from both language instructors and assessment researchers. Owing to the alignment of alternative assessment with the new pedagogical shift to constructivism and technological support, alternative assessment provides both an assessment and a teaching strategy to support students' language learning. In an EFL context, portfolio assessment is increasingly implemented in writing courses due to its capacity to document students' progress and reflection over the course, in addition to the formative function. Nevertheless, the implementation of portfolio assessment in language assessment is not without challenges. The aim of this book chapter is four-fold. First, we review the theoretical basis on which alternative assessment is based on. Second, empirical research on the implementation of portfolio assessment in writing courses will be discussed. Based on these two sections, the conditions for successful implementation of portfolio assessment will be put forward. Finally, recommendation for future research as to portfolio assessment in language teaching will be discussed.

METHODS

Literature Sources

In order to conduct the review, different scientific resources have been consulted, including Google Scholar, Science Direct, Web of Science, SCOPUS, and ERIC. In addition, specific journals focusing on language assessment were checked upon. We did not restrict the year of publication because this is a thematic review, thus year did not play an important role in documenting the evolution of the alternative assessment over the years. However, we restricted the language used to that of English only and only peer-reviewed articles and book chapters were included.

As for keywords, a combination of different phrases focusing on both alternative assessment and portfolio assessment were used. These included "alternative assessment "or "formative assessment" or "writing portfolio" or "portfolio assessment" and "second language (L2) learning" or "EFL setting" or "EFL classroom" or "foreign language teaching."

The search of articles was iterative due to the nature of the research objectives, namely to review the conditions for successful portfolio assessment implementation. Thus, when initial findings from the selected body of articles were revealed, new keywords were derived to fulfil the research objectives. In this case, "portfolio assessment" and "feedback" or "reflection" were entered into the search engine.

A snow-balling approach was also employed, i.e., once a relevant article was found, the researchers consulted the referenced list and the journal in which the article was published to search for more relevant article.

Our searches returned a total of 259 potential papers and book chapters, but after screening their abstracts based on the review focus, only 25 were read in detail. The articles included in the review are marked with an asterisk (*) in the reference list.

FINDINGS

Theoretical Basis of Alternative Assessment

The history of English language teaching has shifted from a more teacher-centered, e.g., Grammar-Translation to student-centered approaches, evident in the communicative approaches to English learning. The former relies on behaviorism which suggests that students can learn by a process of drilling certain language vocabularies and grammatical structures under the teachers' guidance. The latter views each student's progress as varied and exposes them to the learning environment with abundant language cues. In addition, during this learning process, students can receive support and feedback from peers and teachers to make progress. In other words, the approach is based on principles of constructivism which focus on individual differences in knowledge construction and collaboration (Anderson, 1998).

In the teaching and learning of writing skills, for instance, the implementation of constructivism is increasingly advocated because writing is a complicated productive skill and is built upon the accumulated knowledge of the writer. The latter recognizes that each student differs in their learning path to acquire the expected language skills specified by the course. Aligned with this constructive approach, the teachers should design instructions in a way that enables the identification and remediation of students' difficulties (Beck, Llosa, Black, & Anderson, 2018). In other words, the constructivist approach should be accompanied by formative or alternative assessment so as to reach these instructional goals rather than summative assessment, which is more appropriate for differentiation purposes.

At the heart of alternative assessment is the emphasis on students as active learners who are supported to have the ownership of their learning (Lam, 2017). This means they are expected to be self-directed in their learning and be able to set goals, monitor the extent to which these goals are achieved, and have different behavioral, motivational, and metacognitive strategies to optimally fulfil the task at hand (Zimmerman, 2000).

Researchers have found that students' self-regulation is highly contingent on teachers' instructional approach, especially in the case of low-achievers. This necessitates that teachers should provide different types of support and scaffolding during the learning process which students can rely on to manage their own learning. Thus, it is crucial to use different forms of assessment like external feedback from teachers and peers or internal feedback or self-reflection during the learning process rather than one final score from timed-exams organized at the end of the course.

According to Biggs (2003), students are motivated to learn and fulfil learning tasks that are clearly connected to both the learning objectives and assessment tasks. More importantly, students will invest effort in the content and activities that are assessed. This is the principle of constructive alignment which specifies that learning objectives – learning activities – and assessment tasks should be aligned to optimize teaching and learning (Biggs, 2003). Therefore, in order to promote students' self-reflection, the provision of feedback to peers, and the internalization of peer feedback to self-regulate the learning process, teachers should make explicit how these are being assessed and their role in the final assessment. It is only when these activities are recognized and appreciated from an assessment perspective that students will be more involved. This being said, formative assessment is more appropriate when a constructivist approach is employed in the teaching and learning of languages. More importantly, to enhance students' engagement, principles of constructive alignment should also be inherent in the assessment approach.

In this section, how alternative or formative assessment accommodates the pedagogical shift to constructivist approach in language teaching was discussed. In the next section, we will review how portfolio assessment endorsed as a formative assessment approach to the teaching and learning of writing skills of EFL or L2 has an effect on students' writing skills.

The Implementation of Portfolio Assessment in Writing Courses

Portfolio Assessment – An Overview

A portfolio is a collection of various forms of evidence of achievement of learning outcomes. In practical terms, a student portfolio for assessment purposes is a compendium of reports, papers, and other material, together with the student's reflection on his/her learning and strengths and weaknesses (Davis & Ponnamperuma, 2005).

There are two types of portfolios: formative and summative. A formative or learning portfolio documents the stages of learning and provides a progressive record of a student's growth (Burner, 2014). A summative or showcase portfolio demonstrates the mastery of a learning task or a set of learning objectives and contains only the best work (Burner, 2014. Teachers usually use the formative portfolios to help students identify learning goals, document progress over time, and demonstrate learning mastery. In general, teachers use formative portfolios to document the stages that students go through as they learn and progress (Venn, 2000).

According to Burner (2014), a writing portfolio is "a collection of texts which the students has had the opportunity to develop and reflect upon over a long period of time" (p.140). There are three main components in a portfolio: a collection of the different draft and revisions that demonstrate an ongoing learning process, a reflection upon the learning goals, and a selection of works that demonstrate learning mastery (Hamp-Lyons & Condon, 2000). As can be seen, the process of compiling a portfolio, particularly a writing portfolio, necessitates active cognitive and metacognitive engagement on the part of students. In this process, the role of the teachers in stimulating learning activities that enable peer support for revisions and/or self-reflection is indispensable (Burner, 2014).

Empirical Research on the Implementation of Portfolio Assessment in Writing Courses

In the early implementation stage, portfolio assessment in writing is employed as an alternative form of assessment to replace timed essays which usually result in writing anxiety for students. One study found that portfolio assessments could help students could get a higher grade (Elbow & Belanoff, 1986) and another found that the use of portfolios triggers more reflection on the part of the students, which is helpful for teachers to devise informed-decision as to teaching strategies (Camp,1990). Similarly, students are found to be more aware of the task requirements when portfolios are introduced (Murphy & Smith, 1990). These findings suggest that the early implementation of portfolio assessments improves learning outcomes and helps students to learn more effectively than one time summative assessment of writing at the end of a course. Furthermore, the narrowed scope of genre and topic of timed essay administered at the end of the course or in standardized tests may not fully reflect the writing competences of students from diverse in socio-cultural backgrounds. One of the well-mentioned positive effect of implementing portfolio assessment is that learning is evaluated at later stage. Beforehand, students are supported with language forms, genre writing, or the logical flow of argumentation. Thus, their language anxiety is substantially reduced and it becomes less pressing compared to timed-essay assessment (Chen, 2006).

The perceptions of teachers and students regarding the positive effects of portfolios on students' affective and cognitive outcomes are corroborated by later empirical research. Most studies show that portfolio assessment can promote a learner-centered approach to teaching and students' reflection (e.g., Fox & Hartwick, 2011; Little, 2009; Nunes, 2004). In addition, portfolio assessment also helps students to evaluate their own language development and helps motivate them to employ strategies to facilitate their knowledge acquisition (Fox & Hartwick, 2011). Through a process of drafting and revising, the teacher and students can visualize the progress made in learning, and thus better decisions can be made regarding the next steps in learning and the final assessment (Burner, 2014; Hattie & Timperley, 2007). In terms of academic achievement, research has shown that students in portfolio learning conditions outperform peers in the control groups (Baturay & Daloglu, 2010; Cho, 2003; Li; 2010; Nezakatgoo, 2011; Song & August, 2002).

Nevertheless, while researchers are attracted by the ecological and humanistic characteristics of portfolio assessment, its reliability and fairness has been questioned. A number of studies show that when assessed by two different raters, the inter-rater reliability is not so high. For example, Koretz (1998) reports inter-rater coefficients ranging from 0.28 to 0.57 in a large-scale portfolio assessment program. As for fairness, questions have been raised regarding whether students receive the same level of support from peers and instructors when they are assessed under portfolio and non-portfolio conditions, and thus whether one group is disadvantaged relative to the other.

As discussed, the implementation of portfolios is to combine both teaching and assessment to improve teaching pedagogies. This approach to writing teaching has enabled more student-student and teacher-student interaction. Learning writing is now a collaborative process rather than an individual attempt. During this process, both cognitive, i.e., language acquisition, and metacognitive strategies, i.e., how to develop and monitor plans for further improvement, are emphasized. Thus, it is more valuable to reflect upon how to support these cognitive and metacognitive skills during portfolio assessment so that students are capable of making progress as well as the assurance of portfolio being a reliable assessment method.

Conditions for Successful Implementation of Portfolio Assessment in Writing Courses

Feedback

As portfolios are formative in nature, the interactions between teachers and students, and among the students themselves, are of crucial importance. Research has shown that when students are just given tasks, deadlines, and interim feedback, they can hardly take advantage of portfolio assessment (Lam, 2013). Conversely, providing and responding to feedback should be an ongoing process, wherein students can work on the revision of their writing tasks until this results in a satisfactory work before new tasks are assigned (Lam, 2013).

When it comes to feedback, two issues arise. One is whether students can make sufficient use of the feedback from teachers and peers. If this is the case, feedback can help students identify the gap between their current performance and the learning goals, and provide guidance on how to achieve or surpass expected objectives, and how they can improve their work (Bryan & Clegg, 2006). Furthermore, it can provide motivation and direct students' attention towards to self-regulated practice (Delany & Molloy, 2009). Feedback also helps to develop students' reflection and give them a chance to discover errors and find solutions for themselves (Hodgson & Berry, 2011). Another issue is to how to train students to provide qualitative feedback to their peers as well as to make feedback exchanges an interactive process that leads to more cognitive gain, rather than being simply a procedural process.

Students' Capacity in Composing Portfolio

From the history of portfolios, we know that they have mostly been used in fine arts and architecture to display graphical work, and they continue to be widely used in health professions ((Heywood, 2000; Weigle, 2002). These all have to do with pictorial or graphical material. Furthermore, portfolios do not lend themselves easily to being graded – the student is usually required to demonstrate that they have completed a range of tasks and activities to a minimum standard (Miller, 2002). Lam (2017) posits that most students can appropriately compile their artifacts which can be accomplished works to include in a portfolio for grading purposes. Yet, the process through which students can utilize the interim feedback and reflection for further improvement remains unclear.

An essential part of a portfolio is the students' reflection on the learning activities/tasks or practice that they are exposed to during the instructional process and this is usually done through the medium of writing. If reflection is conducted in a proper manner, i.e., without being in fear of displaying weakness or something that may affect the grading by the teacher, it will be more of a recording of events and achievement. It provides not only evidence of students' current progress and achievement, but also helps them to become aware of their own skills, strengths, and limitations as well as serving as an indication for their developmental needs (Priest & Roberts, 1998). However, to what extent reflection provides evidence about mastery and fosters learning depends greatly on the students themselves, namely, their writing skill (proficiency), their mastery of critical thinking skills (Aydin, 2010), their creativity, their past experiences, the depth of their self-reflection, and the purpose of the portfolio (Wenzel, Briggs, & Puryear, 1998). Chang, Wu, and Ku (2005) reported that students found the reflection part of the portfolio the most difficult task. According to Mitchell (1994), students with good writing skills will have more advantages than their peers and usually have a positive feeling towards portfolio assessment. In addition, the quality of reflection also relies on one's prior knowledge. For example, secondary students with more knowledge have been found to be more accurate in the evaluation of their own performance, and make better selections in terms of new learning tasks or extra work for improving their progress (Koston, Van Gog, and Paas, 2010). On the other hand, students sometimes overrate their works and produce unauthentic reflection (Brown & Harris, 2013). This is because the purpose of the portfolio has two paradoxical effects on the part of the students (Driessen, Tartwik, Overeem, Vermunt, & Van Der Vleuten, 2005). On the one hand, if the portfolio is not used for summative assessment, then students tend not to take it seriously or are less likely to use it if no pressure is present, and so it will not be of great use for their achievement over time. But, on the other hand, if it is used for summative assessment, then students may be reluctant to reveal their weaknesses because they know that this will lead to a lower grade. Hence, honesty in a students' portfolio is an important requirement if the teacher is to use it as an assessment tool, especially given that there may be a negative correlation between the use of portfolio and the honesty of students' reflection (Mitchell, 1994).

DISCUSSION AND IMPLICATIONS

Pedagogical Recommendations

Quality Feedback

Quality feedback obviously plays an important role in students' learning process, especially when portfolio assessment is used. Quality feedback needs to provide clear messages that students can understand and use to improve their tasks. It must be descriptive, not judgmental and, especially, must be about students' work, not the student. It should include both positive and negative feedback. Positive feedback focuses on the positive features of learning behavior, skills, qualities and performance, whereas negative feedback provides advice to students on what they need to do to improve (Berry, 2011). Stronge (2007) suggests that quality feedback should relate specifically to the criteria of the task, hence, the feedback can increase students' learning outcomes. Moreover, quality feedback should also be given promptly while pupils are still mindful of the topic, assignment, or performance in question, so that they are more likely to focus on it and use it to improve their learning goals (Fitzwater, 1998).

Feedback can be provided by teachers or peers, depending on the objectives of the teacher and the nature of the task. There is no need for a teacher to give feedback after every task and to every student, as this would be unnecessarily demanding on the teacher's time. According to Gielen et al. (2010), who investigated the effectiveness of peer feedback on 43 students of Grade 7 in secondary education in a Dutch writing course, although peer feedback is not as accurate as that of experts, it can nevertheless have a significant impact on students' improvement, especially those of low-achievers at the first-time of writing.

Alternatively, teachers can implement different instructional strategies to stimulate feedback between students. Gielen, Peeters, Dochy, Onghena, and Struyven (2010) identify five types of instructional interventions that affect the long-term motivation of students. The first type of intervention "can interrupt the natural interaction process by enforcing the use of the same communication structures on all occasions" i.e., teachers utilize direct questions and sentence openers to stimulate comments as well as reflective interaction among the learners. The second type of intervention is training student to comply with specific quality criteria. For the third type of intervention, some researchers believe that there must be a quality control system to filter unreliable feedback (Kali & Ronen, 2008; Cho & MacArthur, 2010). With the purposes to enhance feedback quality and assessee's response, the fourth type focuses on a feedback form prompting the assessor to address these needs in the feedback. The last type of intervention uses a *posteriori* response form to inspire students to reflect on the peer feedback they received and demonstrate how they used the peer feedback to revise their works. Teachers could utilize these different instructional strategies to help students learn how to provide better feedback on the writing of their peers.

One important characteristic of peer feedback is the justification of how a peer reviewer came to such a conclusion, i.e., answer the Why question. Unfortunately, justification is a difficult skill to teach (Gielen, Tops, Dochy, Onghena, & Smeets, 2010). However, it is believed that students can be trained to be skillful if peer feedback giving is conducted frequently with more prompts from teachers regarding the criteria to be assessed for a particular task (Gielen et al., 2010). For those who receive feedback, the teachers can also offer help with a kind of *a posteriori* reply form in which students indicate the extent to which they respond to their friend's feedback as well as what they have learnt when they assess their friend's work with questions like: From the critical comments of my friend, I particularly remember that ..., Assessing the work of somebody else, I learned that ..., After the friend's comment, I revised my work with regard to (criterion) because ... and I tried to solve this by ..., I paid this time special attention to ... since ..., (Gielen et al., 2010). Using this kind of *a posteriori* reply form not only makes students more aware of what they should improve, it also in the long term helps them to become more reflective self-regulated learners, which is considered to be an important skill for their lifelong learning.

Enhance Students' Capacity of Reflection on Learning Achievement and Demonstration

Rubrics provide a useful tool to help students improve their skill in building a portfolio that reflects the learning process and demonstrates their achievement (Anderson, 1998; Margery & Gminda, 2005). These normally specify the criteria for assessment, so that students are well-informed regarding what needs to be included. In portfolio assessment, both the teacher and the students participate in the assessment process. Consequently, it is important for the teacher to establish the criteria and indicate the kinds of evidence students have to include to demonstrate their learning, so in order for students to decide what to include in their portfolio, the teacher should make clear the objectives in every lesson and what kind of evidence is appropriate to demonstrate the competence. Furthermore, the teacher can give examples of common items used in portfolios that are appropriate for the purposes of the course or related to organized learning activities, e.g., minutes of group discussions, a critical description of a good/bad experiences, essays in which they explain, elaborate or reflect on the points they find important or interesting, a one-page report based on their evaluation of the problem they successfully/unsuccessfully solved, or examples of improvements.

In addition, to avoid inaccurate or unfocused reflection, the teachers can suggest questions upon which students can reflect on their achievement. When necessary, the teachers can also organize interviews for under-achieving students or high achievers to provide further explanation. More importantly, Tang and Biggs (1999) suggest that the teacher should avoid using an analytical method to assess portfolios, i.e., the final grade is the sum of all the items. This will not only cause students to select all of their good work to include and all their strengths or achievement, but also is against the spirit of portfolio assessment, because the aim of using portfolio to assess the whole learning process by judging whether the whole performance matches our teaching objectives. Additionally, the teacher can suggest a sampled structure of the portfolio and guidelines so that they can have some concept. However, the guidelines should not be too rigid, so that students have room for creativity. Also, the teacher can set the word limit for each item, e.g., one-page for a summary of interesting points, so that the portfolio is not too extensive and the items are carefully selected to demonstrate the relevance to the learning objectives. Both the teacher and students can discuss which items are compulsory and optional to put in. Regarding the number of items, Biggs and Tang (1998) suggest that it depends on the teaching objectives; however, a four-item portfolio is sufficient for a semester.

Recommendation for Future Research as to Portfolio Assessment in EFL Teaching

Recent research on the use of portfolios in language teaching demonstrates that teaching and assessment can be combined to result in enriched learning experience for students. The core elements for successful implementation of portfolio assessment include teacher and peer feedback, the development of metacognitive skills, self-regulation by students, and the fairness of assessment. Apart from concern about the fairness and/or reliability of assessment, all of the other core elements have been found to be significantly and positively related to learning outcomes in different learning contexts (e.g., Yang, Badger, & Yu, 2006; Filius, Kleijn, Uijl, Prins, Van Rijen, & Grobbee, 2018). Most of the research in this field thus far has been in contexts other than portfolio assessment in language learning. There is great scope for further empirical work on how portfolio assessment can be implemented and used to enhance instructional practices in language teaching and learning. In particular, there is a need to address the issue of the fairness and reliability of portfolio assessment perhaps through the development of common guidelines for indicators that can be used in portfolio assessment to address different stages of language acquisition, the progress made during the learning process, and the authenticity of reflection by students. Furthermore, how these factors should be used for a final assessment needs to be considered from the perspectives of both students and teachers. In doing so, we will have more confidence in the implementation of portfolio assessment in language teaching settings and "it is possibly to rethink portfolio assessment, not to be an alternative form of assessment, but rather a common assessment tool" (Burner, 2014, p. 146).

CONCLUSION

The use of portfolio assessment is more likely to foster a deep approach to learning and help students to become more reflective language learners than more traditional end-of-course summative assessments. In practice, this creates more work for the teacher in providing feedback, grading, and supporting students to compile the learning portfolio. It is also possible that if portfolio assessment is applied, students may not achieve as high scores as they usually get or a fully objective assessment is difficult to be reached. This is inherent in the nature of portfolio assessment. Therefore, some students may favor the traditional assessment methods after experiencing portfolio assessment (Baeten, Dochy, & Struyven, 2008) However, if the school is to advocate a more personalized and constructivist approach to language teaching and learning, portfolio assessment is strongly recommended due to its formative nature and cognitive and metacognitive advantages regarding students' learning.

REFERENCES

Anderson, R. S. (1998). Why talk about different ways to grade? The shift from traditional assessment to alternative assessment. *New directions for Teaching and Learning, 1998*(74), 5-16.

Aydin, S. (2010). EFL writers' perceptions of portfolio keeping. *Assessing Writing, 15*(3), 194-203.

Baeten, M., Dochy, F., & Struyven, K. (2008). Students' approaches to learning and assessment preferences in a portfolio-based learning environment. *Instructional Science, 36*(5-6), 359-374.

Baturay, M. H., & Daloğlu, A. (2010). E-portfolio assessment in an online English language course. *Computer Assisted Language Learning, 23*(5), 413-428.

Beck, S. W., Llosa, L., Black, K., & Anderson, A. T. (2018). From assessing to teaching writing: What teachers prioritize. *Assessing Writing, 37*, 68-77.

Berry, R. (2011). *Assessment Reform in Education: Policy and Practice.* New York: Springer.

Biggs, J. (2003). Aligning teaching for constructing learning. *Higher Education Academy*, 1-4.

Biggs, J., & Tang, C. (1998). Assessment by portfolio: Constructing learning and designing teaching. In P. Stimpson, & P. Morris, *Curriculum and Assessment for Hong Kong: Two components, one system* (pp. 443-462). Hong Kong: Open University of Hong Kong Press.

Brown, G. T. L., & Harris, L. R. (2013). Student self-assessment. In J. H. McMillan (Ed.), *Sage handbook of research on classroom assessment* (pp. 367–393). LosAngeles: Sage.

Brown, S. & Smith, B. (1997). *Getting to Grips with Assessment.* Birmingham: SEDA Publications.

Bryan, C., & Clegg, K. (2006). *Innovation Assessment in Higher Education.* Oxford. Routledge.

Burner, T. (2014). The potential formative benefits of portfolio assessment in second and foreign language writing contexts: A review of the literature. *Studies in Educational Evaluation, 43,* 139-149.

Camp, R. (1990). Thinking together about portfolios. *The Quarterly, 12*(2), 8–14.

Chang, Y. J., Wu, C. T., & Ku, H. Y. (2005). The introduction of electronic portfolios to teach and assess English as a foreign language in Taiwan. *TechTrends, 49*(1), 30-35.

Chen, Y. M. (2006). EFL instruction and assessment with portfolios: A case study in Taiwan. *Asian EFL Journal, 8*(1), 69-96.

Cho, Y. (2003). Assessing writing: Are we bound by only one method?. *Assessing writing, 8*(3), 165-191.

Davis, M. H., & Ponnamperuma, G. G. (2005). Portfolio assessment. *Journal of Veterinary Medical Education, 32*(3), 279-284.

Delany, C., & Molloy, E. (2009). *Clinical Education in the Health Professions: An Educator's Guide.* Chatswoods NSW: Elsevier Australia.

Driessen, E. W., Van Tartwijk, J., Overeem, K., Vermunt, J. D., & Van Der Vleuten, C. P. (2005). Conditions for successful reflective use of portfolios in undergraduate medical education. *Medical education, 39*(12), 1230-1235.

Elbow, P., & Belanoff, P. (1986). Portfolios as a substitute for proficiency examinations. *College Composition and Communication, 37*(3), 336-339.

Filius, R. M., Kleijn, R. A., Uijl, S. G., Prins, F. J., Van Rijen, H. V., & Grobbee, D. E. (2018). Strengthening dialogic peer feedback aiming for deep learning in SPOCs. *Computers & Education.*

Fitzwater, T. (1998). *The Manager's Pocket Guide to Documenting Employee Performance.* Amherst, MA: HRD Press.

Fox, J., & Hartwick, P. (2011). Taking a diagnostic turn: Reinventing the portfolio in EAP classrooms. *Classroom-based language assessment, 25,* 47-61.

Gielen, S., Peeters, E., Dochy, F., Onghena, P., & Struyven, K. (2010). Improving the effectiveness of peer feedback for learning. *Learning and Instruction, 20*(4), 304-315.

Gielen, S., Tops, L., Dochy, F., Onghena, P., & Smeets, S. (2010). A comparative study of peer and teacher feedback and of various peer feedback forms in a secondary school writing curriculum. *British Educational Research Journal, 36,* 143-162.

Gronlund, N. E. (2006). *Assessment of Students Achievement.* Boston: Pearson.

Hamp-Lyons, L., & Condon, W. (2000). *Assessing the portfolio: issues for research, theory and practice.* Cresskill, NJ: Hampton Press.

Hattie, J., & Timperley, H. (2007). The power of feedback. *Review of educational research, 77*(1), 81-112.

Heywood, J. (2000). Practicals, projects, problem-based learning and portfolios. In Heywood J., ed. *Assessment in Higher Education, Practical Guide.* London: Jessica Kingsley Publishers, pp. 316-346.

Hofgson, C., & Berry, M. (2011). *Adventure Education.* Oxford: Routledge.

Koretz, D. (1998). Large-scale portfolio assessments in the US: evidence pertaining to the quality of measurement. *Assessment in Education: principles, policy & practice, 5*(3), 309-334.

Koston, D., Van Gog, T., & Paas, F. (2010). Self-assessment and task selection in learner-controlled instruction: differences between effective and ineffective learners. *Computers & Education, 54,* 932-940.

Lam, R. (2013). Two portfolio systems: EFL students' perceptions of writing ability, text improvement, and feedback. *Assessing Writing*, *18*(2), 132-153.

Lam, R. (2017). Taking stock of portfolio assessment scholarship: From research to practice. *Assessing Writing*, *31*, 84-97.

Li, Q. (2010). The impact of portfolio-based writing assessment on EFL writing development of Chinese learners. *Chinese Journal of Applied Linguistics*, *33*(2), 103–116.

Little, D. (2009). Language learner autonomy and the European language portfolio: Two L2 English examples. *Language teaching*, *42*(2), 222-233.

Margery, H. D., & Gminda, G.P. (2005). Portfolio assessment. *Journal of Veterinary Medical Education*, *32*(3), 279-284.

Miller, N. (2002). Alternative forms of formative and summative assessment. *The Handbook for Economics Lecturers: Assessment, Bristol: Economics LTSN*, http://www.economicsnetwork.ac.uk/handbook.

Mitchell, M. (1994). The views of students and teachers on the use of portfolio as a learning and assessment tool in midwifery education. *Nurse Education Today*, *14*, 38-43.

Murphy, S., & Smith, M. A. (1990). Talking about Portfolios. *Quarterly of the National Writing Project and the Center for the Study of Writing and Literacy*, *12*(2), 1-3.

Nezakatgoo, B. (2011). The Effects of Portfolio Assessment on Writing of EFL Students. *English language teaching*, *4*(2), 231-241.

Nunes, A. (2004). Portfolios in the EFL classroom: disclosing an informed practice. *ELT Journal*, *58*(4), 327-335.

Shibab, J. (2011) The Impact of Assessment on Students Learning. *Procedia- Social and Behavioral Science*, *28*, 718-721.

Song, B., & August, B. (2002). Using portfolios to assess the writing of ESL students: a powerful alternative?. *Journal of second language writing*, *11*(1), 49-72.

Stronge, J. H. (2007). *Qualities of Effective Teachers (2nd ed.)*. Alexandria VA: Association for Supervision and Curriculum Development.

Tang, C., & Biggs, J. (1999). Assessment by portfolio. In D. Watkins, C. Tang, J. Biggs, & R. Kuisma, *Evaluation of the Student Experience Project: Vol. 2. Assessment of University Students in Hong Kong: How and Why, Assessment Portfolio, students' Grading* (pp. 29-78). Hong Kong: Center for the Enhancement of Learning and Teaching.

Venn, J. J. (2000). *Assessing students with special needs (2nd ed.).* Upper Saddle River NJ: Merrill.

Weigle, S. C. (2002). *Assessing Writing. Cambridge Language Assessment Series.* Cambridge: CUP.

Wenzel, L. S., Briggs, K. L., & Puryear, B. L. (1998). Portfolio: authentic assessment in the age of the curriculum revolution. *Journal of Nursing Education, 37,* 208-212.

Wiliam, D. & Black, P. (1996). Meanings and Consequences: A Basis for Distinguishing Formative and Summative functions of assessment? *British Educational Research Journal, 22*(5), 537-48.

Yang, M., Badger, R., & Yu, Z. (2006). A comparative study of peer and teacher feedback in a Chinese EFL writing class. *Journal of second language writing, 15*(3), 179-200.

Zimmerman, B. J. (2000). Attaining self-regulation: A social cognitive perspective. In *Handbook of self-regulation* (pp. 13-39).

BIOGRAPHICAL SKETCHES

Anh Nguyet Diep

Affiliation: Vrije Universiteit Brussel

Education: Ph.D. Educational Sciences

Research and Professional Experience: Blended learning, online interaction, learning performance, social inclusion

Professional Appointments: Post-doc researcher

Chang Zhu

Affiliation: Vrije Universiteit Brussel

Education: Ph.D. Educational Sciences

Research and Professional Experience: Educational Leadership, Didactics, Online learning, Blended learning, Cultural differences

Professional Appointments: Professor

Minh Hien Vo

Affiliation: Can Tho University / Vrije Universiteit Brussel

Education: MSc. Information Systems Development

Research and Professional Experience: Blended learning, Assessment, Student learning, Instructional design

Professional Appointments: Ph.D. researcher

In: Using Alternative Assessment ...   ISBN: 978-1-53615-161-9
Editors: Hoang Yen Phuong et al.   © 2019 Nova Science Publishers, Inc.

Chapter 2

ENGLISH CURRICULUM REFORM AND FORMATIVE ASSESSMENT POLICIES: CROSS-CASE ANALYSIS - IMPLICATIONS FOR ALTERNATIVE ASSESSMENT RESEARCH IN VIETNAM

Thi Van Su Nguyen[*], PhD
School of Foreign Languages, Can Tho University,
Can Tho, Vietnam

ABSTRACT

This chapter highlights advantages of alternative assessment and elucidates why alternative assessment is important for language learning and teaching, and especially for curriculum reform policies. A brief review on potential problems implementing alternative or formative assessment policies in language classrooms is presented. Two reformed language curricula and assessment policies: Chinese College English Reforms and Vietnamese General English Reforms are examined and suggestions for

* Corresponding Author's E-mail: ntvsu@ctu.edu.vn.

future research related to alternative types of language assessments are presented.

Keywords: alternative assessment, EFL curriculum and assessment reform, language assessment policies, NFL2020

INTRODUCTION: ALTERNATIVE AND TRADITIONAL ASSESSMENT

Critics of traditional language testing have indicated major concerns regarding student achievement due to its focus on one 'snapshot' nature which creates a lot of stress for students (Dickli, 2003). Traditional paper and pen language testing techniques such as multiple choice, true-false statements, gap-filling and matching exercises are claimed to be inappropriate for the foreign language classroom curricula. Traditional tests lack rich, descriptive information about both the product and process of language learning (Barootchi & Keshavarz, 2002; Law & Eckes, 1995) and unable to direct students' authentic learning (Bailey, 1998). In addition, the so-called 'washback effect' caused by traditional language testing approaches - has negatively impacted upon the curriculum at both educational and psychological level. Standardized tests force classroom teachers to pay attention to what is tested in the examination and therefore-those standardized tests directly dominate the whole curriculum (Shepard, 1991) and affect the methodology the teachers use in their classes which usually is exam preparation practices (Bailey, 1999; Wall, 1996).

In recent years there has been a shift in language testing-- from psychometric to alternative approaches of assessment. As Hamayan (1995) put it, alternative assessment signifies authentic procedures and techniques within the instructional domain which can be integrated into daily classroom activities. Alderson and Banerjee (2001) believe that alternative assessment provides students with beneficial washback effects, which cannot be gained through traditional testing approaches.

Alternative assessment has been viewed as motivating and inspiring to learners and offers teachers a chance to realize students' weaknesses and strengths (Law & Eckes, 1995). Some alternative assessment types such as performance or authentic assessment present a real-world problem (Elliott, 1995) and enable teachers to make a link between their instruction and the real-world experience through meaningful tasks, and encourage students' higher order thinking skills to solve real-life problems (Simonson, Smaldino, Albright & Zvacek, 2000; Worley, 2001). The other types of alternative assessment, portfolio or projects, on the other hand, emphasize the construction of knowledge for the final product through processes which require problem-solving approaches (Simonson et al., 2000). Diaries, journals, and writing folders are other approaches to alternative assessment which are believed to encourage learners to reflect upon both what they have learned and make links across the curriculum, and to develop students' connection with their teachers (Worley, 2001). Research into alternative assesement is abundant, however, much shifts its focus on individual types of alternative assessment in EFL contexts. Difficulties arise, however, when an attempt is made to implement the alternative assessment policy in the process of curriculum reform or revision. This paper therefore is organised into four sections. First, it introduces alternative and formative assessment incentives as documented in some curriculum policies. The second part focuses on some challenges in the enactment of alternative/formative assessment policies. The two next sections identify how alternative/formative assessment was implemented in two English reformed curricula: the Chinese College English Curriculum and the Piloted Vietnamese General English for Schools Curriculum. The last part discusses the directions for English teacher education in Vietnam regarding assessment training and pinpoints some areas of research that warrant further attention in the field of assessment.

Thi Van Su Nguyen

ALTERNATIVE-FORMATIVE ASSESSMENT AND CURRICULUM POLICIES

Since alternative assessment is ongoing in nature, it becomes possible to focus both on the process and product of learning (Hamayan, 1995). In other words, rather than summative assessment, alternative assessment is termed as alternative approaches to traditional testing techniques, to ensure students' ongoing language developments and to inform teachers' instructions, revision of teachers' teaching practice. In this respect, alternative assessment can be considered as formative assessment - *assessment for learning* and is on-going in nature. In this book, we will use the term *alternative* and *formative assessment* with very similar connotations, to contrast its nature with *summative* or *traditional testing techniques.*

Alternative assessment provides teachers with a platform to link assessment and instruction, allowing teachers to monitor and modify instruction continuously based on what is already assessed. In other words, if the objectives of a set instructional program are met then the process is continued; otherwise, it has to be revised (Genesee & Hamayan, 1994). Therefore, alternative assessment is considered to be more informative, and more advantageous to teachers compared to traditional test scores in terms of helping teachers to redesign the curriculum in a way that is more responsive to students' learning progress (Hamayan, 1995; Worley, 2001). Alternative assessment is a much better platform to foster both teachers and students' reflection on teaching and learning goals, because it encourages appropriate adjustments related to their intended learning outcomes as identified in a curriculum. Due to the advantages in curriculum revisions offered by alternative approaches to assessment, current educational policies have seen huge support for a variety of different types of alternative assessment (Al-Mahrooqui & Denman, 2018; Chen, May, Klenowski & Kettle, 2013; Inbar-Lourie, 2015; Leung & Rea-Dickens, 2007).

POTENTIAL CHALLENGES IN THE ENACTMENT OF ALTERNATIVE/FORMATIVE ASSESSMENT POLICIES

In a recent UNESCO (2017) report on policies for continuous assessment in low-income countries, a range of issues fundamental to the effective implementation and usefulness of continuous assessment in the classroom are identified. The report focuses on successful cases of implementation of continuous classroom assessments and therefore provides insights into directions for alternative assessments of language learning. The paper examines continuous assessment in low-income countries and analyses a few challenges in the implementation of alternative methods to assessment. In those countries examined, "conditions such as very large class sizes, few resources, poorly trained teachers, and a severe triage of students from the formal system—i.e., testing that pushes students out of school—often pose particularly problematic challenges" to continuous assessment (UNESCO, 2017, p. 8). In language assessment, similarly, it has been warned that the current incentives for alternative types of assessment as regulated in national language policies are not implemented as they should be in reality. Inbar-Lourie (2015) has reviewed the discrepancies between policies for alternative assessment and the implementation of those policies into language classroom practices. A few countries were examined as case studies in this review, including UK, Canada, Denmark, Hongkong and China. In most of the reviewed cases, there are big gaps between the policy and the practice of alternative forms of assessment. More research on the implementation of alternative assessment needs to be conducted to resolve current challenges between the policies, incentives to continuous assessment and the practice of those assessment types. It has been pointed out that the practical implementation of alternative assessment in traditionally hierarchical societies, such as those found in certain parts of Asia, should be taken with great cautions, due to the socio-cultural characteristics and testing habits of the area (Al-Mahrooqui & Denman, 2018). The following sections will look closely at two cases, China and

Vietnam, in the enactment of the reformed English curriculum and its testing and assessment policies.

THE CHINESE ALTERNATIVE/FORMATIVE ASSESSMENT POLICY: THE COLLEGE ENGLISH CURRICULUM REFORM

The Chinese authorities have implemented their Chinese English curriculum policy through a series of documents and explicit guidelines for curriculum and assessment. The Chinese Ministry of Education introduced The College English Curriculum Requirements (CECR) in 2007, including policies related to continuous assessment. It is recommended that the inclusion of formative assessment into the existing summative assessment framework of College English is necessary. This policy was said to potentially change the nature of assessment and its role in the teaching and learning of English in Chinese universities (Chen, May, Klenowski & Kettle, 2013). Under the new CECR framework, the textbooks, the content and format of testing and assessment were revised. Teachers were not only required to change their teaching approaches, but also to alter their teaching philosophies and beliefs. Concerns have been raised regarding its feasibility and appropriateness in the Chinese context, which has been dominated by a long tradition of examinations (Carless, 2011; Chen, 2009; Cheng, 2008).

The Chinese reform in terms of assessment has been extensively researched and a few constraints and obstacles in the implementation of the alternative assessment types such as self-assessment or peer-assessment were raised. The first obstacle was the difficulty in attempting to establish top-down formative assessment removed from classroom realities in a testing culture (Gu, 2014). The next concern is the fact that the incorporation of a formative assessment component (by the Ministry of Education) in the College English Curriculum Requirements causes discrepancies between policy and classroom realities (Chen, May, Klenowski & Kettle, 2014). In addition, there were issues related to teachers' lack of language assessment literacy and professional development such as support of and engagement with other teachers, just as in Western countries (Inbar-Lourie, 2015). Yu (2015), on the other hand, found that students were skeptical about the usefulness of peer-feedback that was not teacher-initiated. Students' reliance on the teacher as the ultimate authority and the implementation of peer-feedback thus reflects the difficulty of moving toward a more genuine role for students in classroom assessment practices. This points to the need for students to be more meaningfully engaged self-editing and peer-feedback activities in order for the policy intent to be fully realised. Yu (2015) concluded that the major impetus for the reform of English policy is how teachers make sense of and enact the reform. Without localised management from school leaders and teachers, formative assessment policies might not be sufficient to ensure change in practice (Yu, 2015). This is in line with Gu's (2012) suggestion about the Chinese authorities' guidelines in terms of language curriculum and assessment, emphasizing that teacher assessment literacy is one crucial factor in the assessment reform.

The Chinese approach to English curriculum reform and alternative assessment policies has contributed to recent debate in the implementation of formative and alternative assessment policies in current teaching practice. Firstly, just as Hill & Barber (2014) highlighted, the implementation of *assessment for learning* principles and practices usually lags far behind the declared policies and this turns to be also the case of Chinese language testing and assessment reform. In many other cases where formative and alternative assessment types are implemented, the lack of clarity as to what is meant by formative assessment principles and practices inhibits the implementation (Inbar-Lourie, 2015). Therefore, it is suggested that teacher formative assessment literacy needs to be addressed at local level, if successful implementation of assessment policy is to be realised in certain Asian countries, where the testing culture has rooted for such a long time (Al-Mahrooqi & Denman, 2018).

THE VIETNAMESE REFORMED CURRICULUM AND ASSESSMENT POLICY: THE PILOTED GENERAL ENGLISH FOR SCHOOLS

In 2008, the government in Vietnam promulgated the policy entitled the National Foreign Languages Project 2008-2020 (commonly known as NFL2020, Decision 1400, or Project 2020). The intended outcome of NFL2020 is to provide Vietnamese students of all educational levels with a good command of foreign language (Decision 1400, 2008) so that by 2020 the majority of Vietnamese youths graduating from colleges and universities will have sufficient language proficiency to use language independently and confidently in communication in their working environment and in a globalized and multi-cultural environment (Decision 1400, 2008).

The NFL2010 has a variety of specific objectives: implementing the ten-year General English curricula (from Grade 3 to Grade 12), replacing the current seven-year General English curricula, implementing the reformed English curricular for vocational colleges, and universities, and reforming the teaching and learning of English for language teachers, and improving language proficiencies for language teachers, other teachers and employees.

Under the NFL2020, the reformed General English curriculum textbooks (seven-year curricula) was initiated as a part of the project, with the overall aim of reforming the current General English textbooks and curricula. Decision 1400/QD-TTg on the approval of the national project entitled "Teaching and learning a foreign language in the national education system, Period 2008-2020," three pilot English curricula for Vietnamese schools were designed and promulgated by the Vietnamese Ministry of Education and Training (MOET):

- Pilot English Curriculum for Vietnamese Primary Schools
- Pilot English Curriculum for Vietnamese Lower Secondary Schools
- Pilot English Curriculum for Vietnamese Upper Secondary Schools

In late 2010-, MOET assigned Vietnam Educational Publishing House to organize the development and production of the ten-year English textbook series for Vietnamese Schools (from grade 3 to grade 12) in collaboration with two publishers – MacMillan Education and Pearson Education. In accordance with the instructions on how to implement the piloted curriculum for General English textbooks, instructions on how to evaluate students are modified accordingly. In particular, the types of General English assessments have recently been promulgated in details in the official dispatches: CV7972/BGDĐT-GDTrH or CV5333/BGDĐT-GDTrH. In those documents, formative assessments have been specified as compulsory for each school semester. At least four times of formative assessment need to be conducted per semester for English, in addition to summative assessments (Circular 58/2011/TT-BGDĐT). Government official dispatches also suggest certain types of alternative assessment that teachers might consider in their language classes. For example, it is stated:

> All schools must administer both formative and summative assessment according to specific guidelines as indicated in Circular 58/2011/TT-BGD-DT (12/12/2011) (MOET). The assessment must encompass four language skills and language focuses. Formative assessment should be used mainly for speaking skills. Students are evaluated formatively in class with some guided alternative assessment types such as: giving short answers to teachers' questions, story-telling, presenting and debating on a topic, topic-based discussion, discussion, interviewing, role-playing in pair, or groups, and other activities. It is important to focus on students' communicative competence and conversational skills. Students must be assessed formatively at least two times per semester. (CV7972, MOET, 2011, pp. 3-4)

Similarly, for all three levels (primary, lower secondary and upper secondary), formative assessment is required and regulated in similar documents. Vietnam is long famous for its testing cultures, the new regulations for formative assessment, therefore, might pave its way to encourage new developments in the teaching and learning of English in Vietnam under the reformed contexts.

While current National Language Project and the general pilot curricula have received more attention lately in the research agenda, the implementation of the new approaches to testing and assessment aligning with the pilot curricula has not yet been well researched. The implementation of NFL2020 has radically impacted language education in Vietnam (see for example, Le, Nguyen & Burns, 2017; Nguyen, 2015; Nguyen, 2018). As briefly reviewed, the piloted curricula to General English in Vietnam is very attentive to aligning the communicative competence goals and assessment types and activities. A curriculum focusing on tests was gradually replaced by a curriculum stimulating both formative and summative assessment. Initial internal results of the research have shown that teachers' evaluations of the textbooks are very positive (Hoang, 2015). However, issues related to the implementation of alternative types of assessment are rarely discussed in the research agenda. Will the pilot English curriculum reform in Vietnam face the same challenges as Chinese reform because the two education systems tend to depend heavily on test culture? Or as in some Western countries, is there a mismatch between policy and implementation of alternative assessment for language classrooms in Vietnam? What needs to take into account when designing alternative assessment types in Vietnamese language classes? To what extent can teachers' professional development training help improve teachers' alternative assessment literacy? These questions should be answered before the pilot curricula becomes official.

IMPLICATIONS FOR TEACHER TRAINERS AND RESEARCHERS IN VIETNAM

The new language policies in both the Chinese case and the Vietnamese case have certainly led to changes in the ways language teachers teach and assess students. Incentives to adopt formative, on-going approaches to language assessment are encouraged and highlighted in the reformed curricula. While Chinese policies to encourage alternative types of assessment have been researched extensively at both policy level and classroom level as mentioned earlier, few attempts have been made in the Vietnamese context. Some studies have been done, such as portfolio assessment by Duong, Nguyen, Griffin (2011) or the Confucian heritage influence on formative assessment (Thanh-Pham, & Renshaw, 2015; Thanh-Pham, 2013). However, few research has shifted its focus on how alternative or formative assessment is formulated in the reformed General English curriculum. The relationship between incentives policies and practice of alternative types of assessment remain unanswered. Although recent research into the Vietnamese reformed English Curriculum under the National Project 2020 has been abundant in terms of developing teachers' English proficiency (Le, Nguyen & Burns, 2017) and teachers' professional developments (Nguyen, 2018), few studies have investigated how the Project changes teachers' competence in assessing students. Neither students' nor teachers' response to new types of assessment has been taken into account.

Research from Chinese and even some Western contexts has indicated that although policies to formative assessment and/or alternative assessment are very supportive, there tend to be strong discrepancies between policy and practice. Problems associated with class size, testing cultures, teachers' pedagogical knowledge are all constraints to the implementation of alternative assessments in EFL classroom contexts. Whether those problems persist in Vietnamese EFL classrooms remain to be uncovered. This chapter focuses on one particular context where there is active discussion over reform of the English curriculum, but still alternative assessment is not gained equivalent attention. While the literature of how EFL assessment policies have met current practice is increasing to bridge the gaps between policy and the practice of assessment, further research is needed into the implementation of EFL formative assessment under the new policy to General English programs in Vietnam.

Researching formative or alternative assessment will not only help to revise the current implementation of the pilot English curriculum, but is also meaningful for teacher trainers, and local teachers in the process of reforming English program in Vietnam. Future researchers can question the implications of types of alternative assessment not only at tertiary level, but secondary contexts as well. Teacher trainers can consider the types of training that aligning curriculum outcomes, teaching and learning activities and assessment types (alternative inclusive), rather than just focusing on principles of language teaching.

REFERENCES

Alderson, J. C. & Banerjee, J. (2001). Language testing and assessment (Part 1). *Language Teaching, 34 (4),* 213-236.

Al-Mahrooqi, R., & Denman, C. (2018). Alternative Assessment. In J. I. Liontas (Ed.), *The TESOL Encyclopedia of English Language Teaching* (pp. 4851-4856). Hoboken, NJ: Wiley.

Barootchi, N., & Keshavarz, M. H. (2002). Assessment of achievement through portfolios and teacher-made tests. *Educational Research, 44*(3), 279-288.

Bailey, K. M. (1998). *Learning about language assessment: dilemmas, decisions, and directions.* Heinle & Heinle: US.

Bailey, K. M. (1999). *Washback in Language Testing.* TOEFL Monograph Series MS-15. Princeton, NJ: Educational Testing Service.

Carless, D. (2011). *From testing to productive student learning: Implementing formative assessment in Confucian heritage settings.* New York, NY: Routledge.

Chen, Q. (2009). The potential barriers to college English assessment policy change in China: A sociocultural perspective. In B. Garrick, S. Poed & J. Skinner (Eds.), *Educational planet shapers: Researching, hypothesising, dreaming the future* (pp. 115 126). Brisbane: Post Pressed.

Cheng, L. (2008). The key to success: English language testing in China. *Language Testing, 25,* 15–37.

Chen, Q., Kettle, M., Klenowski, V., & May, L. (2013). Interpretations of formative assessment in the teaching of English at two Chinese universities: a sociocultural perspective. *Assessment & Evaluation in*

Higher Education, 38(7), 831-846. doi:10.1080/02602938.2012. 726963.

Chen, Q., May, L., Klenowski, V., & Kettle, M. (2014). The enactment of formative assessment in English classrooms in two Chinese universities: Teacher and student responses. *Assessment in Education: Principles, Policy & Practice, 27*(3), 271-285. doi:http://dx.doi.org/10.1080/ 0969594X.2013.790308.

CMOE. (2007). *College English Curriculum Requirements.* Beijing: Higher Education Press.

Dikli, S. (2003). Assessment at a distance: Traditional vs. alternative assessments. *The Turkish Online Journal of Educational Technology, 2*(3), 13–19.

Duong, M.T., Nguyen, C., and Griffin, P. (2011). Developing a Framework to Measure Process-orientated Writing Competence: A Case Study of Vietnamese EFL Students' Formal Portfolio Assessment. *RELC Journal (Journal of Language Teaching and Research), 42*(2), 167-179.

Elliott, S. N. (1995). Creating meaningful performance assessments. *ERIC Digest* E531.

Ewing, S. C. (1998). Alternative assessment: popularity, pitfalls, and potential. *Assessment Update, 10* (1), 11-12.

Genesee, F., & Hamayan, E. (1994). Classroom-based assessment. In F. Genesee (Ed.), *Educating Second Language Children* (pp. 212-239). Cambridge: Cambridge University Press.

Gu, P. Y. (2014). The unbearable lightness of the curriculum: what drives the assessment practices of a teacher of English as a Foreign Language in a Chinese secondary school? *Assessment in Education: Principles, Policy & Practice, 21*(3), 286-305. doi:10.1080/0969594X.2013. 836076.

Gu, Y. (2012). English curriculum and assessment for basic education in China. In J. Ruan & C. Leung (Eds.), *Perspectives on teaching and learning English literacy in China* (pp. 35–50). Dordrecht, Netherlands: Springer.

Hamayan, E. V. (1995). Approaches to Alternative Assessment. *Annual Review of Applied Linguistics, 15*, 212-226.

Hill, P. & Barber, M. (2014). *Preparing for a Renaissance in Assessment.* London: Pearson.

Hoang, V.V. (2015). Teachers' Evaluation of Primary English Textbooks for Vietnamese Schools Developed under the National Foreign Language 2020 Project: A Preliminary Internal Survey. *VNU Journal of Science: Education Research, 31*(4), 1-15.

Inbar-Lourie, O. (2015). Bridging the policy-practice-formative assessment gap: A language-assessment-literacy perspective. *Paper presented at the EALTA Conference, Copenhagen.* Retrieved http://www.ealta.eu. org/conference/2015/presentations/Friday/Friday%20Morning%20Bef ore% 20Coffee% 20Break/ EALTA % 202015 % 20Ofra %20 Inbar-Lourie.pdf.

Law, B. & Eckes, M. (1995). *Assessment and ESL.* Peguis publishers: Manitoba, Canada.

Le, D.M., Nguyen, T.M.H, & Burns, A. (2017). Teacher Language Proficiency and Reform of English Language Education in Vietnam, 2008-2020. In D. Freeman & L. Le Dréan (Eds.), *Developing Classroom English Competence: Learning from the Vietnam Experience* (pp. 19-33). Phnom Penh: IDP Education (Cambodia).

Leung, C., & Rea-Dickins, P. (2007). Teacher Assessment as Policy Instrument: Contradictions and Capacities. *Language Assessment Quarterly, 4*(1), 6-36. doi:10.1080/15434300701348318.

MOET. (2008). *Decision No. 1400/QĐ-TTg: Teaching and Learning Foreign Languages in the National Education System, Period 2008 to 2020.* Retrieved from http://www.chinhphu.vn/portal/page/portal/ chinhphu/ hethongvanban?class_id=1&_page=18&mode=detail&docu ment_id=78437.

MOET. (2012). *Quyết định 5209 về việc ban hành Chương trình giáo dục phổ thông môn Tiếng Anh thí điểm cấp Trung học phổ thông.* [*Decision 5209/2012/TT-BGDĐT on the promulgation of the piloted General English curriculum for secondary students*] Retrieved from https:// thuvienphapluat.vn/ van-ban/Giao-duc/Quyet-dinh-5209-QD-BGDDT-nam-2012-Chuong-trinh-giao-duc-pho-thong-mon-tieng-Anh-180993. aspx.

MOET. (2011). *Thông tư 58/2011/TT-BGDĐT về Quy chế đánh giá, xếp loại học sinh trung học cơ sở và học sinh trung học phổ thông.* [*Circular 58/2011/TT-BGDĐT on regulation on assessment and classification of secondary school and high school assessing and evaluating secondary students*]. Retrieved from https://thuvienphapluat.vn/van-ban/Giao-duc/Thong-tu-58-2011-TT-BGDDT-Quy-che-danh-gia-xep-loai-hoc-sinh-trung-hoc-co-so-133268.aspx.

MOET. (2013). *Công văn số 7972/BGDĐT-GDTrH v/v hướng dẫn triển khai chương trình GDPT môn tiếng Anh thí điểm cấp trung học theo Đề án "Dạy và học ngoại ngữ trong hệ thống giáo dục quốc dân giai đoạn 2020* [*Official Dispatch 7972/BGDĐT-GDTrH on the instructions for piloted upper and lower secondary piloted English Curriculum under the Teaching and Learning Foreign Languages in the National Education System Project 2020*]. Retrieved from https://thuvienphapluat.vn/cong-van/Giao-duc/Cong-van-7972-BGDDT-GDTrH-2013-giao-duc-pho-thong-mon-tieng-Anh-thi-diem-cap-trung-hoc-245291.aspx.

MOET. (2014). *Công văn số 5333/BGDĐT-GDTrH v/v triển khai kiểm tra đánh giá theo định hướng phát triển năng lực môn tiếng Anh cấp trung học từ năm học 2014-2015.* [*Official Dispatch 5333/BGDĐT-GDTrH on the implementation of testing and assessment for General English secondary schools according to competency-based orientation since 2014-2015*]. Retrieved from https://thuvienphapluat.vn/cong-van/Giao-duc/ Cong-van-5333-BGDDT-GDTrH-phat-trien-nang-luc-mon-tieng-Anh-2014-2015-288353.aspx.

Nguyen, V. T. (2018). Project 2020 and professional development for high school EFL teachers in Vietnam. In K. Hashimoto & V.T. Nguyen (Eds.), *Professional Development of English Language Teachers in Asia.* London: Routledge.

Nguyen, H. N. (2015). Vietnam's national foreign language 2020 project: challenges, opportunities and solutions. In S. Sharbawi & T. W. Bigalke (Eds.), *English for ASEAN integration: policies and practices in the region* (pp. 62-64). Brunei: University Brunei Darussalam. Retrieved from http://bruneiusprogramme.org/2013- forum-publication.

Shepard, L. A. (1991). Will national tests improve student learning? *CSE Technical Report 342, CREEST*, University of Colorado, Boulder.

Simonson, M., Smaldino, S., Albright, M. & Zvacek, S. (2000). Assessment for distance education (ch 11). *Teaching and Learning at a Distance: Foundations of Distance Education.* Upper Saddle River, NJ: Prentice-Hall.

Thanh-Pham, T. H. (2013). *Implementing Cross-culture Pedagogies - Cooperative Learning at Confucian Heritage Cultures.* Dordrecht: Springer.

Thanh-Pham, T. H., & Renshaw, P. (2015). Formative assessment in Confucian heritage culture classrooms: activity theory analysis of tensions, contradictions and hybrid practices. *Assessment & Evaluation in Higher Education, 40*(1), 45-59. doi:10.1080/02602938.2014.886325.

UNESCO. (2017). *In-Progress Reflection No. 13 on Continuous Assessment for Improved Teaching and Learning: A Critical Review to Inform Policy and Practice.* Current and Critical Issues in Curriculum, Learning and Assessment. Retrieved from http://unesdoc.unesco.org/images/0025/002555/255511e.pdf (Accessed 10 July 2018).

Wall, D. (1996). Introducing new tests into traditional systems: insights from general education and from innovation theory. *Language Testing, 13* (3), 334-354.

Worley, T. M. (2001). Alternative assessment: methods to make learning more meaningful. *Presented at Pathways to Change: International Conference on Transforming Math and Science Education.* Retrieved on April 16, 2018 from http://www.academia.edu/21567771/alternative _assessment_methods_to_make_learning_more_meaningful.

Yu, A. (2015). A Study of University Teachers' Enactment of Curriculum Reform in China. *International Education Studies, 8*(11), 113-121.

BIOGRAPHICAL SKETCH

Thi Van Su Nguyen

Affiliation: Can Tho University

Education: PhD

Research and Professional Experience: Higher education teaching and learning, academic development, language teachers' professional development, formative assessment, teaching L2 writing.

Professional Appointments: Lecturer

Publications from the Last 3 Years:

- Nguyen, T. V. S., & Laws, K. (2019). Changes in higher education teachers' perceptions of curriculum. *Journal of Applied Research in Higher Education*, *11*(1), 76-89. Doi:10.1108/JARHE-06-2018-0097.
- Nguyen, T. V. S., & Laws, K. (2016b). *Higher Education Teachers' Conceptions of Teaching: Are Changes Feasible?* In T. Doe & K. Sell (Eds.), Practitioners as Researchers: Case Studies of Innovative Practice (pp. 70-85). Sydney, Australia: Primrose Hall Publishing.
- Nguyen, T. V. S., & Laws, K. (2016a). Higher Education purposes through teachers' lenses: perspectives from Vietnam. *Journal of Teaching and Education (JTE)*, 5(1).

Thi Van Su Nguyen holds a Bachelor Degree in Language Education (Can Tho University, Vietnam), a Master (TESOL) and a PhD Degree in Education (both from the University of Sydney, Australia). Her PhD thesis was a grounded theory exploration of university teachers' conceptual changes on teaching and learning. Su has coordinated a few teachers' professional development projects funded by World Bank, and AusAid,

Thi Van Su Nguyen

which aim to develop in-service teachers' teaching and research competence.

Su has presented papers in some education conferences such as SRHE (UK), HERDSA (Australasia), and become members OCIES (Oceania), and DEPISA (Southeast Asia). Currently she is based in Can Tho, Vietnam working as an English teacher trainer for both pre-service and in-service language teachers. She is interested in researching L2 language writing, L2 teachers' identity and formative assessment. Her research area also includes higher education teaching and learning, teachers' identity, and academic development.

In: Using Alternative Assessment …   ISBN: 978-1-53615-161-9
Editors: Hoang Yen Phuong et al.   © 2019 Nova Science Publishers, Inc.

Chapter 3

THE USE OF SELF-ASSESSMENT TO IMPROVE EFL STUDENTS' SPEAKING PERFORMANCE: A REVIEW

Quyen Thi Thanh Tran[*]
Department of General English and English for Specific Purposes
Can Tho University, Can Tho, Vietnam

ABSTRACT

Together with the changes in learning and teaching pedagogies, alternative assessment methods are becoming more and more appreciated in educational practice. Self-assessment is one form of alternative assessment and has been suggested as a reliable and valid method for assessing students' communicative competence. In this book chapter, a review of self-assessment in speaking skills is examined. A thematic literature review was conducted on the benefits of self-assessment in speaking skill, tools to self-asasess students' speaking skills and empirical research on validity and effects of self-assessment on students' speaking performance. The review showed (1) contradictory ideas on the use of self-assessment and that (2) studies on the effects of self-assessment on

[*] Corresponding Author's E-mail: thanhquyen@ctu.edu.vn.

students' speaking skills in the English as a foreign language (EFL) context. Pedagogical implications and recommendations for further studies in the field are suggested.

Keywords: self-assessment, speaking skills, effects of self-assessment on students' speaking performance

INTRODUCTION

English is considered an international language which has been used in all fields including international relations, science, business, tourism and culture (Majanen, 2008). Therefore, the importance of English in non-English speaking countries, especially in the globalization era nowadays, is motivating educators and researchers to seek teaching techniques and innovations to help learners communicate effectively in English. Indeed, for communication purposes, speaking is considered the most important skill which should be given appropriate control and assessment based on students' speaking proficiency (Burnkart, 1998, cited in Nazara, 2011).

Apart from teaching methods, assessment in language teaching and learning also has great impacts on the learners' learning process. Indeed, assessing the learners' oral production is the central concern of various scholars (Celce-Murcia, 2013; Louma, 2004). In a learning process, learners need to know their abilities, their weaknesses, how much progress they have made, and what they should do with the skills they have acquired. By involving learners in the assessment process, they learn the qualities needed for good performance, how to judge their own performance or achievement, how to set personal goals, and finally they develop the habit of self-reflection (Rolheiser and Ross, 1998). Therefore, teachers should provide students opportunities to assess their learning.

However, traditional assessment methods are very limited in providing students such opportunities to reflect on their learning. Yorke, (2001) claims that the use of conventional tests with marks early on can have a detrimental impact on students. This becomes a more serious and problematic matter as

Littlewood (1999) observed that East Asian students expect the teacher, as the holder of authority and knowledge, to be responsible for the learning assessment. To avoid these drawbacks, new methods of assessment should be introduced into the language classroom to improve learners' learning outcomes and teaching effectiveness.

Self-assessment, one form of alternative assessments, has recently gained significant attention in foreign language education settings because of its apparent benefits. These include encouraging greater effort, boosting self-confidence, facilitating awareness of distinctions between competence and performance, and enhancing self-awareness of learning strengths and weaknesses (Blue, 1994). Hunt, Gow, and Barnes (1989, p. 207) even claim that without learner self-evaluation and self-assessment 'there can be no real autonomy'. Especially, Bachman and Palmer (1989) conclude that the self-assessment could be a reliable and valid method for assessing communicative competence.

However, there has been some debates on whether learners can or cannot assess their speaking ability (Ross, 1998; Saito, 2008). This question needs further research. In addition, there are still limited studies of learner involvement in the assessment of speaking skills and the effect of self-assessment on students' speaking performance in the English as a foreign language context (EFL), apart from the recent studies of Ariafar and Fatemipour (2013) and Charif & Chekroun (2017). In the Vietnamese context, very few studies have attempted to explore the use of self-assessment in assessing students' speaking skills even though alternative assessment has gained more recognition recently.

Thus, this review on the effects of self-assessment on students' speaking skills will first contribute to the need of literature on one form of alternative assessment in EFL contexts: self-assessment in speaking performances. Second, practical implementations on self-assessment techniques and considerations suggested in the review will provide EFL teachers with guidance, which can be applied in similar teaching settings. In addition, gaps identified in this review will appeal further studies, especially those investigating the effect of self-assessment on students' speaking skills as well as other language skills.

Quyen Thi Thanh Tran

This review consists of three parts. First, it will define self-assessment accompanied with its related benefits and concerns. Second, it will describe some literature about self-assessment in speaking skills. Finally, relevant studies on the effects of self-assessment on students' speaking skills will be carefully reviewed.

METHODS

To explore the research trend in self-assessment of students' speaking skills in English language teaching, a content analysis approach was employed. This review collected data through different online sources, mostly Google Scholar with the focus on article journals about the effects of EFL students' self-assessment on their speaking performance. Since this is a thematic review, there was no restriction on the year of the paper publication. Key words related to the research theme include self-assessment, speaking self-assessment, speaking performance and the effects of self-assessment on students' speaking performance. A total of 101 potential papers and book chapters were consulted, but only 37 of them were selected for inclusion in this review because they were relevant to and aligned with the research theme.

FINDINGS

Self-Assessment in Language Teaching

Saito (2003) claims that "the current trends in learner-centered language teaching approaches, and a growing interest in instructiveness and authenticity have led to a greater interest in expanding the use of second language self-assessment" (p. 1). In fact, self-assessment is one form of alternative assessment and is a process through which students learn about themselves (Dikel, 2005). Brown and Hudson (1998) divide self-assessment into three types, performance self-assessment, comprehension self-assessment and observation self-assessment. This review focuses mainly on self-assessment of speaking performance in foreign language teaching and learning settings.

Self-assessment is aligned with constructivism theory, in which individuals actively construct knowledge, rather than acquire it passively (Glasersfeld. 1989). The practice of self-assessment; therefore, creates a setting for students to actively engage in discussions of how their learning performance will be evaluated and what desired performance consists of, leading to reflection on what they have achieved. Practical implementation requires learners to be trained carefully in self-evaluation based on specific criteria.

Criteria for Effective Self-Assessment

In order to apply self-assessment techniques effectively, several criteria should be taken into consideration. Indeed, learners' ability to self-assess effectively develops over time and with experience (Cassidy, 2007). According to Chamot and O'Malley (1994), "self-assessment requires the student to exercise a variety of learning strategies and higher order thinking skills that not only provide feedback to the student but also provide direction for future learning" (p. 119). Chappelle and Brindley (2002) summarize major principles of self-assessment practice comprising of the importance of providing students with training in the use of self-assessment techniques; ability to self-assess should not be taken for granted; the transparency of the assessment instrument impacts accurate self-assessment. Besides, self-assessment scales are most effective when statements are situations specific and have a close relation to students' personal willingness to self-assess and also the accuracy of that assessment may be affected by cultural factors.

Moreover, in order to increase the effectiveness of self-assessment and engage students in assessment to activate deep learning, several essential factors should be considered: clear criteria, training, intervention and feedback, and sufficient practice (AlFallay, 2004; Chen, 2006 and Patri, 2002). Most importantly, clear criteria should be given to students in advance because as long as students are aware of the criteria for success, assessment is valid (Airasian, 1997; Stiggins, 2001).

Thus, self-assessment which follows constructivism theory is quite compatible with the learner-centered approach emphasized in language teaching and learning nowadays. Yet, the important thing is that the practice of self-assessment is effective only if it meets specific principles and criteria together with a need of discussion between the teacher and students on these criteria prior to practice.

Benefits of Self-Assessment

A review on self-assessment reveals a strong acknowledgement of its benefits so far. Rolheiser and Ross (1998, p. 10) give four reasons why self-assessment should be applied in the language classroom. First, self-evaluation will focus student attention on the objectives measured. Second, the assessment provides teachers with information they would otherwise lack. Third, students will pay more attention to the assessment. Finally, student motivation will be enhanced. They also believe that self-assessment is "unique" in asking learners to reflect on their performance (p. 10). However, learners are able to assess their abilities more accurately when provided with specific self-assessment statements which are closely related to their personal experience (Ross, 1998).

Recent studies confirm the benefits of self-assessment. For example, Charif and Chekroun (2017) describe three major merits of self-assessment: (1) increasing students' interest and motivation to think about their own learning progress and problems so that they can find ways and strategies to improve; (2) helping students to develop critical and meta-cognitive skills for analysis of their own work; and (3) probably minimizing the fear and anxiety students' face before the tests and exams. The important point is that self-assessment is a useful skill for students' life-long learning (Boud, 2000 and Puhl, 1997). Indeed, self-assessment is a key learning strategy for autonomous language learning, enabling students to monitor their progress, relate learning to individual needs and open their view about language learning.

However, there has also been some criticism of the use of self-assessment in teaching and learning. For example, Coombe and Canning (2002) state that self-assessment has been one of the more problematic areas of self- directed learning and has been criticized for reasons such as learners' lack of experience to make judgments in self-assessment. In addition, some studies show that it is difficult for some learners to cope with self-assessment techniques; therefore, learner training should be guided to have an effective practice (Lim, 2007).

While the literature on self-assessment reveals both potential benefits and drawbacks associated with its use, on balance, the benefits of self-assessment outweigh its disadvantages. Its merits can be summarized as enhancing students' academic achievement, learning motivation, strategic learning or life-long learning skills, autonomous learning, critical and meta-cognitive skills and even lowering learning anxiety, which are key factors leading to the success of language learners. Most of the problems with self-assessment can be avoided through learner training and practice. Therefore, implementing self-assessment in language learning is quite promising and productive to boost learners' academic achievement

Using Self-Assessment in Speaking Skills

Benefits

With the great potential of self-assessment, this section intentionally reviews and tries to link self-assessment in speaking skills. Then, some self-assessment speaking tools are also described and analyzed for further practices and consideration.

According to Bachman (1990), with the advent of communicative language teaching, communicative teaching and communicative assessment have become interdependent. In the same vein, Hymes (1974, cited in Buck, 2001) states that the assessment of oral skills is ensured when learners practice producing the target language appropriately and meaningfully in a variety of social situations which are real-life situations and relevant to the lives of the learners, such as role-plays, games, interviews, problem solving activities, and the like. In other words, assessment not only plays an important role on students' oral language learning, but also for communicative purposes in real-life. Indeed, a number of studies stress the utility of performance assessment in making decisions about the students' progress, and in obtaining information about their own learning process (Jones & Tanner, 2008; Murray, 2006; Nitko & Brookhard, 2007; Stiggins, 2008).

In addition, studies on self-assessment in language learning have examined the value of self-assessment in different language skills. Underhill (1987) introduces self- assessment as a test type which can be used for involving learners in the assessment of their spoken language, and refers to it as "the easiest, cheapest, and quickest form of assessment" (p. 22). However, the process of speaking assessment is considered as very contentious and intricate (O'Sullivan, 2008), which requires a profound understanding of assessment criteria so the learners' ability to accurately assess self or peers' oral performances has often been challenged. Although in order to self-assess oral performance effectively, careful consideration, designs, preparations and practices should be done, this form of assessment brings a lot of benefits in return. Babaii et al. (2015, p. 11) emphasize that the use of speaking self-assessment can (1) increase students' self-awareness and detection of weak points followed by improved learning; (2) have the positive influence of the use of speaking scoring criteria on the accuracy of self-assessment; and (3) lead to the long-lasting effect of self-assessment, in comparison with teacher assessment and on-going learning.

Self-Assessment Tools for Speaking

There are a variety of tools for speaking self-assessment, including rubrics, checklists, rating scales, video, video recording, ect… Rubrics are widely used for assessing proficiency in different tasks (Brown, 1998) and can provide an assessment that is more comprehensive than provided by standardized testing (Arter & McTighe, 2001). There are two types of rubrics e.g., holistic rubrics and analytic rubrics. The former scores the overall quality, proficiency, or understanding of the specific content and skills without judging the component parts separately (Moskal, 2000). While they are quick and convenient for informal testing (Thornbury, 2005), they are difficult to assign scores consistently because few students meet one description accurately and they do not yield feedback on students' strengths and weaknesses. However, this type of rubric is not suitable for formative assessment as it does not provide specific feedback on areas that need improvements in students' oral performance. In contrast to holistic rubrics, analytic rubrics score for separate, individual parts of the performance, followed by a summed total score and give feedback to students regarding how to improve their performance (Mertler, 2001).

There are also two approaches to assess students' speaking performance comprising of analytic and holistic one. In terms of rubrics, analytic rubrics help students get specific feedback on their produced output and keep track of the learners' speaking proficiency development; and provide information about their own areas of strengths, weaknesses and learning needs. Meanwhile, holistic rubrics are scoring guidelines upon which raters base their general and overall impression of the level or quality of the learners' speaking proficiency without a detailed feedback (Moskal, 2000; Andrade, 2000). As far as rating scale is concerned, rating scales with holistic descriptors are the most commonly used self-assessment technique (North, 2000). It could be because it is easier and less time-consuming to assess students' speaking ability as whole. Most importantly, Huot (1990b) raises the point that holistic scoring may be more valid than analytic scoring because it is a more authentic method of assessing communication. The sum of the analytic parts does not necessarily equal the whole response because it isolates linguistic features from context (Goulden, 1994, as cited by Barkaoui, 2011). Thus, depending on specific purpose and students' levels, teachers can choose the appropriate self-assessment speaking tool as well as the approach to assess their performance.

In many respects, checklists similar to rubrics and can work equally well for guiding self-assessment, depending on the assignment (Andrade and Valtcheva, 2009). Stricklands et al. (2000) note that checklists can be used as a formative tool to record data during assessment or as a summative tool to make evaluations, based on collected data. In other words, a checklist is an effective self-assessment speaking tool which can be used flexibly and conveniently in both a summative or formative way. Rating scales are similar to checklists except that they indicate the degree of accomplishment with scales rather than just yes or no; and they can be utilized holistically or analytically as well.

A video recording portfolio is also a way to assess and review students' oral performance; this allows students to view and reflect on their communication and body language. Then they can rate their performance according to the rating criteria provided that they can know their mistakes and weaknesses. This allows them to overcome their difficulties and develops their performance.

Generally, each tool has its own benefits. Andrade (2000) supports the usefulness of rubrics to help students become more thoughtful judges of the quality of their performance and those of their peers. For teachers, they can save time and make evaluating student performance faster and easier. Anderson (2003) adds that rubrics help students in goal-setting and planning, which are crucial metacognitive strategies, thus supporting students' learning. Indeed, self-assessment through rubrics help students understand and evaluate their own performance and that of their peers, reducing arguments among students. Checklists also help students to become self-reliant, self-directed and self-assessing learners (Huba and Freed, 2000). In other words, with a checklist, students can know exactly what they have done and what is missing. However, they are limited to providing feedback with yes or no statements, without much detail on how to make improvement.

As a whole, this section elaborates how relevant self-assessment is used to assess students' speaking performance accompanied with a description and evaluation of various self-assessment tools. In the next section, how self-assessment endorsed as a formative assessment approach to the teaching and learning of speaking skills of EFL or L2 and its effect on students' speaking performance will be reviewed.

Research on the Use of Self-Assessment in EFL Students' Speaking Performance

Seven studies are selectively chosen for careful review in this section to describe the overall pictures of how previous studies examined the use of self-assessment to assess students' speaking skills, especially the effect of self-assessment on students' improvement of their speaking performance, which is the main focus of this review.

Research on the Validity of Speaking Self-Assessment

In the first example, Ibberson (2012) conducted a study to compare the learners' use of checklists and rubrics. The participants were fourteen learners of English in a university in the U.K. The researcher attempted to explore the validity of the two self-assessment tools devised with the Common European Framework of Reference for Language (CEFR) for spoken production. The checklist had one statement per each CEFR level so that the participants could simply check one of the two choices: able to use or difficult to use. The second was an analytic rubric based on the four constructs (range, accuracy, fluency, and coherence) defined in the CEFR for spoken production. The participants were trained to use both types of self-assessment tools to rate their own recording. The rating data was collected each week. The result showed that by the fifth week, the agreement between the teachers' rating and self-rating reached 73.7% when using the analytic rubric, which was a considerably high level of agreement in comparison to 42.2%, when using the checklist. The researcher, then suggested that a well-devised analytic rubric has a positive effect in generating self-assessment ratings.

However, other studies on the correlations between teachers' and students' rating scores or evaluation show various results. Babaii, Taghaddomi, and Pashmforoosh (2015) found that there was a lack of consistency between learners' self-assessments and those of the teacher, indicating that self-assessment is unreliable as a method of accurate proficiency measurement. Conversely, Griffee (1998) has reported a positive correlation between students' self-assessment and teachers' evaluations, particularly among higher-level learners. Tavakoli (2010) also found high correlations among self-rating and self-classroom assessment, teacher-rating and teacher-classroom assessment, and self-assessment and teacher-classroom assessment. He concluded that alternative assessment such as self- assessment is likely to be as reliable and as valid as performance testing.

Research on the Effects of Self-Assessment on Students' Speaking Performance

Up to now, there appear to be very few assessments of the effects of self-assessment on students' speaking performance. One of the most relevant studies is that of Ariafar and Fatemipour's (2013) who investigated the effect of self-assessment on the speaking skill of 60 pre-intermediate Iranian EFL learners. The research instruments included pre- and post-speaking tests, questionnaire and an analytic rating scale as a self-assessment tool for data collection and treatment. This tool consisted of six criteria e.g., appropriateness, adequacy of vocabulary for purpose, grammatical accuracy, intelligibility, fluency, relevance and adequacy of content. The results revealed that self-assessment practices helped the participants improve their speaking ability. In addition, the authors found that the participants thought positively about the use of self-assessment and showed their willingness to continue using self-assessment. Thus, superficially, this study tends to confirm the effectiveness of using an analytic rating scale as a self-assessment tool to improve students' speaking performance. However, although this study had a very well-designed method to triangulate the data, the sample size of 60 learners was quite small and only 30 learners were directly involved in the intervention. Clearly, then, there is a need for further studies of the effectiveness of using an analytic rating scale as a self-assessment tool to improve students' speaking performance

Macari (2017) investigated the view of tourism graduate students on self-assessment for oral presentation group projects in the English for tourism course at a university in Romania. The participants were 59 first year graduate students. Data were collected through students' personal portfolios and self-reflection. The results indicated that after the course, respondents increased their ability to identify the difficulties they had encountered and to propose amendments, which helped learners develop self-reflective skills and built a supportive community for those who felt insecure about working in a team and speaking to an audience in a foreign language. Generally, the combination of both peer and self-assessment in the presentation project makes the portfolio more diversified for data collection. However, the questionnaire just examined students' perception on self-assessment only. In addition, although the results are quite useful, this study just focused on oral presentation skills and team work skills for a project in the tourism course rather than students' speaking performance in particular.

In the context of Vietnam, Phan and Phuong (2017) carried out a study to investigate students' perception and challenges about the implementation of analytic rubrics for speaking self-assessment. Ninety-eight students from a high school in Vietnam participated in the study. A thirty-four-item questionnaire of the five-point Likert scale was administered to the students to collect data. The result indicated that the students had positive perceptions toward the use of analytic rubrics for their self-assessment. The study also revealed students' problems in using this tool although they did not have a clear perception of the drawbacks of the rubric. This study can be significant to explore speaking self-assessment in a Vietnamese high school context, which has very few studies conducted in this field so far. However, this study just stops at investigating students' perception, showing a gap for more experimental research.

As a whole, it can be seen from the literature that although there are several studies related to the field of self-assessment, they tend to compare the correlation between teachers' and students' speaking rating scores with conflicting results. There is also a diversity in terms of self-assessment employed mainly e.g., rubric, rating scale, portfolio and so on. In addition, the past literature as reviewed in this chapter has overlooked the effects of self-assessment on EFL students speaking improvement with very limited participants and lack empirical experimental studies. This indicates an urgent need of more studies conducted in the field, especially, in a Vietnamese teaching context, where alternative assessment is in its infancy.

DISCUSSION AND CONCLUSION

Notwithstanding some conflicting evidence, the overall benefits of using self-assessment of speaking skills are clear. To be specific, it helps to enhance students' academic achievement, learning motivation, strategic learning or life-long learning skills, autonomous learning, critical and meta-cognitive skills and even lowering learning anxiety. The main obstacle to wider implementation is learners' lack of experience to make judgments in self-assessment and the challenge of coping with self-assessment techniques. However, these problems can be tackled through proper training and practice (Lim, 2007).

There is sufficient evidence to demonstrate the benefits of self-assessment in teaching and learning to justify its wider adoption. However, care needs to be taken in implementation to ensure that the specific tools used (e.g., rubrics, checklists, portfolios, etc.) are appropriate for the task, and that students are trained to use them correctly.

There is a need for further detailed studies on how best to implement the process of self-assessment as a mechanism to foster EFL speaking skills. These studies need to involve a wider range institutions and learner levels, and should include both quantitative and qualitative data collection methods. In addition, further work is need to devise reliable self-assessment tools.

REFERENCES

Airasian, P. W. (1997). *Classroom assessment*. New York: McGraw-Hill.

AlFallay, I. (2004). The role of some selected psychological and personality traits of the rater in the accuracy of self- and peer-assessment. *System*, 32, 407–425.

Anderson, N. J. (2003). Metacognition in writing: Facilitating writer awareness. In A. Stubbs & J. Chapman (Eds.), *Rhetoric, uncertainty, and the university as text: How students construct the academic experience* (10-30). Regina: Canadian Plains Research Center, University of Regina.

Andrade, H. (2000). Using rubrics to promote thinking and learning. *Educational Leadership*, 57(V): 13-18.

Andrade, H. & Valtcheva, A. (2009). Promoting Learning and Achievement through Self-Assessment. *Theory into Practice*, 48(I): 12–19.

Ariafar, M. & Fatemipour, H. R. (2013). The Effect of self-assessment on Iranian EFL learners' speaking skill. *International Journal of Applied Linguistics & English Literature*, 2(IV): 7-13.

Arter, J. & McTighe, J. (2001). *Scoring rubrics in the classroom: Using performance criteria for assessing and improving student performance.* New York: Corwin Press.

Babaii, E., Taghaddomi, S. & Pashmforoosh, R. (2015). Speaking self-assessment: Mismatches between learners' and teachers' criteria. *Language testing*, 33(III): 411-437.

Bachman, L. & Palmer, A. S. (1989). The construct validation of self-ratings of communicative language ability. *Language Testing*, 6, 14-25.

Bachman, L. F. (1990). *Fundamental Considerations in Language Testing.* Oxford: Oxford University Press.

Barkaoui, K. (2011). Effects of marking method and rater experience on ESL essay scores and rater performance. *Assessment in Education: Principles, Policy & Practice*, 18(III): 279–293.

Blue, G. M. (1994). Self-assessment of foreign language skills: Does it work? *CLE Working Papers*, 3, 18-35. Retrieved Aug, 23rd, from http://www.eric.ed.gov.

Bostwick, R. M. & Gakuen, K. (1995). Evaluating Young EFL Learners: Problems and Solutions. *In J.*

Brown, D. & Yamashita, S. O. (Eds.), *JALT Allied Materials Language Testing in Japan*, (57-65). Tokyo: The Japan Association for Language Teaching.

Boud, D. (2000). Sustainable assessment: Rethinking assessment for the learning society. *Studies in Continuing Education*, 22(II): 151-167.

Brown, J. D. (1998). *New ways of classroom assessment.* Alexandria, VA: TESOL Incorporated.

Brown, J. D. & Hudson, T. (1998). The alternatives in language assessment. *TESOL Quarterly*, 32(IV): 653-675.

Buck, G. (2001). *Assessing listening*. Cambridge: Cambridge University Press. https://doi.org/10.1017/CBO9780511732959.

Cassidy, S. (2007). Assessing 'inexperienced' students' ability to self-assess: Exploring links with learning style and academic personal control. *Assessment & Evaluation in Higher Education*, 32(III): 313-330.

Celce-Murcia, M. (2013). Teaching English in the context of world Englishes. In M. CelceMurcia, D. M. Brinton, & M. A. Snow (Eds.), *Teaching English as a Second or Foreign Language*, (4th ed, pp. 2-14). Boston, MA: National Geographic Learning/Cengage Learning.

Chamot, A. U. & O'Malley, J. M. (1994). *The CALLA Handbook: Implementing the cognitive language learning approach.* Implementing the cognitive language learning approach. Reading, MA: Addison Wesley.

Chapelle, C. A. & Brindley, G. (2002). Assessment. In Schmitt, N. (Ed.), *An introduction to applied linguistics*, (pp. 267-288). London: Arnold.

Charif, D. & Chekroun, S. (2017) *Self-assessing Speaking Skill among EFL Students Case of Second Year EFL Students at Tlemcen University*. MA Dissertation.

Chen, Y. M. (2006). Peer and self-assessment for English oral performance: A study of reliability and learning benefits. *English Teaching and Learning*, 30(IV): 1–22.

Cohen, D. K. & Hill, H. C. (2000). Instructional policy and classroom performance: The mathematics reform in California. *Teacher's College Record*, *102*, 294-343. https://doi.org/10.1111/0161-4681.00057.

Coombe, C. H. & Canning, C. H. (2002). *Using self-assessment in the classroom: Rationale and suggested techniques*. Retrieved July 7, 2008 from: http://www3.telus.net/linguisticsissues/selfassess2.html.

Dikel, M. R. (2005). *A guide to going online for self-assessment tools*. Retrieved November 15, 2005, from: // www.rileyguide.com/ assess. html.

Glasersfeld, E. von. (1989). "Cognition, Construction of Knowledge and Teaching." *Synthese*, 80(I): 121-140.

Griffee, D. T. (1998). Classroom self-assessment-A pilot study. *JALT Journal*, *20*(1), 115-125.

Huot, B. (1990b). Reliability, validity and holistic scoring: What we know and what we need to know. *College Composition and Communication*, 41(II): 201–213.

Huba, M. E. & Freed, J. E. (2000). *Learner-centered assessment on college campuses: Shifting the focus from teaching to learning.* Boston: Allyn & Bacon.

Hughes, R. (2002). *Teaching and researching speaking.* New York: Pearson Education.

Hunt, J., Gow, L. & Barnes, P. (1989). Learner self-evaluation and assessment – a tool for autonomy in the language learning classroom. In V. Bickley (Ed.), *Language teaching and learning styles within and across cultures*, (pp. 207–217). Hong Kong: Institute of Language in Education.

Ibberson, H. (2012). Can Learners Self-assess Their Speaking Ability Accurately? *Multilingual Theory and Practice in Applied Linguistics*, 81-84.

Jones, S. & Tanner, H. (2008). *Assessment: A practical guide for secondary teachers (2nd ed.).* London: Continuum.

Khusnia, A. N. (2015). Strategies to enhance peer feedback and self-assessment in extended speaking course. *PEOPLE: International Journal of Social Sciences*, ISSN 2454-5899, 1(I):1334-1344.

Lim, H. (2007). A study of self- and peer-assessment of learners' oral proficiency. *CamLing Proceedings*, 169-176. Retrieved from the Web April 20, 2008. http://www.ling.cam.ac.uk/camling/Manuscripts/ CamLing2007_Lim.pdf.

Littlewood, W. (1999). Defining and developing autonomy in East Asian contexts. *Applied Linguistics*, 20(I): 71–94.

Luona, S. (2004). *Assessing speaking.* Cambridge: Cambridge University Press.

Macari, I. O. (2017). Graduates' self-assessment of their oral presentations of group projects: An EFL case study in Romania. *Issues in Educational Research*, 27(III).

Majanen, S. (2008). English as a lingua franca: teachers' discourses on accent and identity. Unpublished MA Thesis, University of Helsinki. Matsuda, A. (2003). Incorporating World English in teaching English as an international language. *TESOL Quarterly*, 37(IV).

Mertler, Craig A. (2001). Designing scoring rubrics for your classroom. *Practical Assessment, Research & Evaluation*, 7(XXV).

Moskal, B. M. (2000). Scoring rubrics: What, when and how? *Practical Assessment, Research & Evaluation*, 7(III). Retrieved from http://PAREonline.net/getvn.asp?v=7&n=3.

Murray, S. (2006). *The role of feedback and assessment in language learning*. Rhode University, Grahamstown.

Nazara, S. (2011). Students' perception on EFL speaking skill development. *Journal of English teaching*, 1(I), 29-43.

Nitko, A. J. & Brookhart, S. M. (2007). *Educational assessment of students*, (5th ed.). Upper Saddle River, NJ: Pearson Education.

North, B. (2000). *The Development of a Common Framework Scale of Language Proficiency*. New York: Peter Lang Publishing, Inc.

O' Sullivan, B. (2008). *Modelling Performance in Oral Language Tests: Language Testing and Evaluation*. Frankfurt: Peter Lang.

Phan, T. X. & Phuong, H. Y. (2017). Using Analytic Rubric for Speaking Self-Assessment: EFL Students' Perceptions and Challenges. *IOSR Journal of Research & Method in Education*, 7(III): 34-39.

Patri, M. (2002). The influence of peer feedback on self and peer-assessment of oral skills. *Language Testing*, 19(II): 109–131.

Pinner, R. S. (2016). Trouble in paradise: Self-assessment and the Tao. *Language Teaching Research*, 20(II): 181-195. doi: 10.1177/1362168814562015.

Puhl, C. A. (1997). Develop, not judge: Continuous assessment in the ESL classroom. *English Teaching Forum*, 35(II): 2-9.

Rolheiser, C. & Ross, J. A. (1998). Student self-evaluation: What research says and what practice shows. *Center for development and learning.* Retrieved December, 2011, from http://www.cdl.org/.

Ross, S. (1998). Self-assessment in language testing: A meta-analysis and analysis of experiential factors. *Language Testing,* 15(I): 120.

Saito, Y. (2003). The use of self-assessment in second language assessment. *TESOL Web Journal,* 3(I).

Saito, H. (2008). EFL classroom peer assessment: Training effects on rating and commenting. *Language Testing,* 25(IV): 553-581.

Stiggins, R. J. (2008). *An introduction to student-involved assessment FOR learning.* New Jersey: PearsonMerrill Prentice Hall.

Stiggins, R. J. (2001). *Student-involved classroom assessment (3rd ed.).* Upper Saddle River, NJ: Merrill.

Strickland, K. & Strickland, J. (2000). *Making Assessment Elementary.* Portsmouth: Heinemann, 2000.

Tavakoli, (2010). Investigating the relationship between Self- assessment and teacher assessment in academic contexts: A Case of Iranian university students. *Asian EFL JO,* 1, 234-260.

Thornbury, S. (2005). *How to Teach Speaking.* England: Pearson Education Limited Longman.

Underhill, N. (1987). *Testing spoken language: A handbook of oral testing techniques.* Cambridge: Cambridge University Press.

Yorke, M. (2001). Formative assessment and its relevance to retention. *Higher Education Research and Development,* 20(II): 115-126.

BIOGRAPHICAL SKETCH

Tran Thi Thanh Quyen

Affiliation: Department of General English and English for Specific Purposes, School of Foreign Languages, Can Tho University, Vietnam

Education:

University of Can Tho, Can Tho City, Vietnam

M.A. Principles and methods in English language teaching in English (2013)

Thesis Title: "An investigation into Vietnamese teachers' beliefs and practices and students' beliefs about teaching reading in EFL classrooms"

University of Can Tho, Can Tho City, Vietnam

B.A. English Education in English (2009)

Research and Professional Experience:

She has conducted and published research on flipped classroom and action research. Her interests include Computer-assisted language learning, Service learning, Project-based learning and action research. She has been teaching different courses comprising of English listening, speaking, writing and reading skills, General English and English for Tourism courses.

Professional Appointments: Lecturer

Honors:

Can Tho University research grant in 2018. Research project entitled "An evaluation on the effectiveness of a support English program for English-medium instruction courses in an EFL setting".

CamTESOL (Cambodia TESOL) Regional ELT Research Grants Program. The 14th Annual CamTESOL Conference on English Language Teaching, Phnom Penh, Cambodia, February 10th-11th 2018. Research project entitled "Implementing mobile applications: students' perceptions and its effect on the improvement of students' listening skills".

CamTESOL Regional ELT Research Grants Program. The 13rd Annual CamTESOL Conference on English Language Teaching, Phnom Penh, Cambodia, February 18th-19th 2017. Research project entitled "Service Learning integration in ESP courses: its impacts on students' life skills development and academic achievement".

Certificate of Honor: Good Laborer – lecturer having many achievements in a school year from 2016 to 2017, rewarded by the Rector of Can Tho University on August 24, 2017.

Mekong TESOL Research Grant. The 1st Mekong TESOL international conference, Gia Viet English Center and University of Wollongong, January 17th 2016. Research project entitled "Using Podcast Learning Project to Improve non-English majored students in the Mekong Delta Region".

Certificate of Merit: "Good at Work and at Home" in a school year from 2015 to 2016, rewarded by the Chair of the Labor Union, Can Tho University in December 8th 2016.

Certificate of Honor: Good Laborer – lecturer having many achievements in a school year from 2014 to 2015, rewarded by the Rector of Can Tho University in August 31st 2015.

Certificate of Honor: "Good at Work and at Home" in a school year from 2014 to 2015, rewarded by the Chair of the Labor Union, Can Tho University in December 8th 2015.

Certificate of Honor: Good Laborer – lecturer having many achievements in a school year from 2013 to 2014, rewarded by the Rector of Can Tho University in July 28th 2014.

Certificate of Honor: Good Laborer – lecturer having many achievements in a school year from 2012 to 2013, rewarded by the Rector of Can Tho University in August 12th 2013.

Publications from the Last 3 Years:

Tran, T. T. Q. & Nguyen, V. L. (2018). Flipped model for improving students' English speaking performance. *Can Tho University Journal of Science, 54*(2), 90-97.

Tran, T. T. Q. (2017). Students' perception of Flipped model on Facebook for educational purposes. *IOSR Journal of Research and Method in Education*, (7), 7-14.

Tran, T. T. Q. (2016). Investigating the students' practices and perceptions on the podcast learning project for educational purposes. *Depisa*, (4), 183-194.

Tran, T. T. Q. (2015). Improving students' oral presentation skills through principles and models. *Monograph Can Tho*, (1), 53-59.

In: Using Alternative Assessment ...   ISBN: 978-1-53615-161-9
Editors: Hoang Yen Phuong et al.   © 2019 Nova Science Publishers, Inc.

Chapter 4

PERFORMANCE-BASED ASSESSMENT: IMPLICATIONS TO ENGLISH LANGUAGE CLASSROOMS

Quyen Phuong Vo[*]

Department of English Language and Culture
Can Tho University
Can Tho City, Vietnam

ABSTRACT

Performance-based assessment has long been advocated as an alternative to traditional standardized testing in EFL education, owing to its strength in measuring students' actual abilities to respond to real-life language tasks. However, there remain some challenges in validating performance-based assessment outcomes, which have hindered its wider adoption. In this chapter I outline some fundamental aspects of performance-based assessment, in particular its definition, its underpinning philosophies and characteristics, and some positive and negative washback effects. The chapter concludes by analysing the implications of using

---

[*] Corresponding Author's E-mail: vpquyen@ctu.edu.vn.

performance-based assessment to assess student performance in English language classrooms.

Keywords: performance-based assessment, English language classrooms

INTRODUCTION

The emergence of communicative approaches to second language teaching since 1980 has brought new perspectives in language teaching (ELT), language learning, and testing and assessment (Canale & Swain, 1980), with a focus on real-word situations and the actual performance of learners (Brown, 2004; Chinda, 2009; Darling-Hammond and Adamson, 2013; Watson, 2006). With respect to testing and assessment, there are sound arguments for the wider adoption of performance-based assessment in lieu of more traditional standardized tests, in order to encourage learners to improve their performance of the target language (Colley, 2008; Koné, 2015; Volante, 2004).

Performance-based assessments (PBAs) have been used since the 1990s to test a wide range of English language tasks and skills, mainly because of concerns that traditional standardized testing does not involve real-world tasks and thus lacks authenticity (Brown, 2004). Other drawbacks of traditional standardized achievement tests are that they are not effective in assessing critical thinking, problem solving, or other higher order skills (Brown, 2004; Haney & Madaus, 1989; Herrera et al., 2013; Lynch, 2003; O'Neil, 1992; Pierce, 2002), that they do not allow students to present a comprehensive picture of what they know or are able to do in content areas (Surmadi, 2017), and that they provide limited information to teachers on what changes are needed to improve learning outcomes and support the needs of individual students (Espinosa, 2015). For these reasons, there is growing interest in integrating performance-based and other alternative forms of assessment more widely into English language classrooms.

This chapter details several fundamental aspects of performance-based assessments (PBAs) that require consideration. The first part of the chapter deals with definitions and underpinning philosophies and the second part focuses on its major characteristics. The next part describes positive and negative washback effects, and the chapter concludes with a discussion of some implications of assessment practices based on students' performance in English language classrooms.

DEFINITIONS AND PHILOSOPHIES OF PERFORMANCE-BASED ASSESSMENT

Performance-based assessments (PBAs) have been defined in different ways. A useful broad definition might be that they "represent a set of strategies for the ... application of knowledge, skills, and work habits through the performance of tasks that are meaningful and engaging to students" (Hibbard et al., 1996, p. 5). From the perspective of student engagement in learning outcomes, PBAs are a set of strategies that require students to use their knowledge and skills to create a product or perform a task that is authentic and meaningful to them based on certain predetermined criteria (Brown and Hudson, 1998 (p. 662); Stiggins, 2001). Relating to the process of performance, Yu (2014) defines PBAs as the measurement of skills or performance that reflect real-world situations and needs English language learners to develop their original responses explaining their performance processes so as to achieve the expected results. As a consequence, performance tasks are considered as a valid means of assessment in the Common European Framework of Reference for Languages since performance is defined as the production of language in a relatively authentic situations of work or study (Council of Europe, 2001). By comparison with traditional standardized tests, therefore, PBA-designed tasks require students to actively perform various forms of problem-solving exercise rather than passively select answers from traditional standardized tests (Chun, 2010).

Extant literature identified various philosophies for PBAs; however, the two widely-accepted theoretical foundations are Krashen's Comprehensible

Input Hypothesis (Krashen, 1981) and Vygostky's social interaction (as cited in Espinosa, 2015). With respect to the former, Krashen (1981) explains that learners can improve and progress their language learning if they are taught with second language input which goes beyond the choice of words and involves presentation of context, explanation, rewording of unclear words, the use of visual cues and meaning negotiation. This is what PBAs actually bring to language learners. In other words, through the process of PBAs, language learners are offered more opportunities to demonstrate their knowledge and skills in authentic contexts of the target language and then construct their own language learning experiences.

Another theoretical foundation for PBAs is Vygotsky's social interaction (Espinosa, 2015). In particular, Vygotsky mentions that learners can learn through their interactions and communications with others, so teachers can create a learning environment that maximizes their learners' ability by involving them in discussion, collaboration and feedback. This idea is supported by Espinosa (2015) who claims that the vital role of social interaction is revealed in the learning process of English language learners as they construct the new language through socially mediated communication. Hence, this theoretical foundation is likely to be closely linked to PBAs in terms of the evaluation of students' performance in communicative skills in real contexts of social interaction.

CHARACTERISTICS OF
PERFORMANCE-BASED ASSESSMENT

As discussed earlier, performance-based assessments aim to assess learners' performance via their implementation of tasks or projects. Significant features of PBAs will be presented in the following section.

As one of the advocates of PBAs, Wiggins (1989) explains some key elements to be considered in designing PBAs, namely (a) having collaborative elements, (b) being contextualized and complex, (c) measuring real-world tasks, and (d) having standards that are authentic and clear to students.

With more specific analysis, Norris et al., (1998) distinguish PBAs from other types of tests with three basic characteristics: (1) examinees must perform tasks, (2) the tasks should be as authentic as possible, and (3) success or failure in the outcome of the tasks which must usually be rated by qualified judges. Therefore, they detail some typical features of PBA-designed tasks, the appropriateness of raters and rating scale, and other supporting factors for PBAs. In particular, Norris et al., (1998, pp 9-10) detail these characteristics as follows:

These tasks should:

- be based on needs analysis including student input in terms of rating criteria, content, and contexts;
- be as authentic as possible with the goal of measuring real-world activities;
- include collaborative elements that stimulate communicative interactions;
- be contextualized and complex;
- integrate skills with content;
- be appropriate in terms of number, timing, and frequency of assessment; and
- be aligned with the daily actions in the language classroom.

With respect to the appropriateness of raters and the rating scale, the authors clarify that raters should be appropriate in terms of (1) number of raters; (2) overall expertise, and (3) familiarity and training in use of the scale. Additionally, the rating scale should be based on appropriate categories of language learning and development, appropriate breadth of information regarding learner performance, and appropriate standards that are both authentic and clear to students. Therefore, PBAs should be combined with other methods of collecting information, such as self-assessments, portfolios, conferences, or classroom behaviors to maximize PBAs' reliability, validity and accountability.

Brown and Hudson (1998) state that performance assessments have three requirements:

- Examinees are required to perform some sorts of task;
- The tasks must be as authentic as possible; and
- The performances will typically be scored by qualified raters.

Consequently, several features should be considered during the process of performance-assessment. Generally, six typical features of PBAs should be considered (O'Malley and Valdez Pierce, 1996; cited in Brown, 2004, p. 255):

- Students make a constructed response.
- They engage in higher-order thinking, with open-ended tasks.
- Tasks are meaningful, engaging, and authentic.
- Tasks call for the integration of language skills.
- Both process and product are assessed.
- Depth of a student's mastery is emphasized over breadth.

Despite not outlining fundamental characteristics of PBAs in a specific way, later views share the same concern about PBA-designed activities in English language classrooms. In particular, Gorp and Deygers (2014) explain that when teachers develop activities to observe and assess their learners' performance, these activities should highlight what these learners can actually do with the target language. Supporting this view, Shehadeh (2012) insists the PBA activities are also required to engage learners in the real use of the target language. For these reasons, assessing learners' tasks and projects should be carried out during the process of learners' performance rather than their final products only (Koné, 2015).

In general, drawing from the above characteristics of PBAs, important questions relating to the implementation of PBAs are how PBA tasks should be administered, what roles the raters should have and what rating scales look like. These aspects greatly contribute to the value of PBAs in achieving the extended outcomes of English language teaching and learning. In other words, the more carefully the steps in preparing PBAs are carried out, the more reliable and valid the PBAs' outcomes will be addressed in terms of their quality and impacts on both teaching and learning. As a result, it is advisable to thoroughly check the discussed aspects for the effective implementation of PBAs.

WASHBACK EFFECTS OF PERFORMANCE-BASED ASSESSMENTS

Strengths of Performance-Based Assessments

Performance-based assessments have been demonstrated to have its beneficial effects on both English language learners' achievement and on teachers' instruction. From a learner perspective the principal advantage of PBAs compared to traditional standardized tests is that they provide more valid measures of learners' abilities to respond to real-life language tasks, offer better estimates of learners' true language abilities, and allow more reliable predictions of learners' future performances in real-life language situations (Brown and Hudson, 1998). With more focus on learner engagement, learners with different language backgrounds are allowed to engage in cognitively complex activities such as generating strategies, monitoring work, analyzing information, and applying reasoning skills (Bass et al., 2002), thereby enhancing their chances to engage with language production and learning (Goldschmidt et al., 2007). Compared to traditional testing forms, PBA activities also offer more opportunities for English language learners to express their knowledge in a broader sense than the limited linguistic opportunities given to them in traditional multiple-choice (Abedi, 2010; McTighe & Ferrara, 2011; Surmadi, 2017). As a result, PBAs can be considered as an effective way of promoting the application of knowledge and skills in situations that closely resemble those of the real world (Kirmizi & Komec, 2016; McTighe & Ferrera, 1998; Wiggins, 1998). In other words, through PBAs, students' understanding and reasoning are constantly tested to determine how well they can apply what they know from what they learn (Glisan et al., 2007; Herrera et al., 2013). Consequently, PBAs can be considered a less anxiety-inducing method students more time to produce and edit their work (Kirmizi & Komec, 2016). Additionally, students are motivated to put in greater effort when they perform in real contexts (Abedi, 2010; Kone, 2015; McTighe & Ferrara, 2011). As a result of the higher level of motivation obtained from performance assessment, English language learners progress more rapidly in their academic endeavors.

With regard to the impacts of PBAs on English language teachers, this type of assessment provides teachers with information about how their learners understand and apply knowledge so as to provide them with more learning experiences (Brualdi, 1998). By using performance assessment, teachers are able to directly observe how well learners apply desired skills and knowledge (McTighe & Ferrara, 2011; Espinosa, 2015). Therefore, PBAs can not only provide immediate feedback for teachers to construct their daily teaching practices in accordance with their students' learning styles, but also help diagnose the students' strengths and weaknesses related to classroom instruction in support of their learning (Pierce, 2002).

Downsides of Performance-Based Assessments

Despite the beneficial effects of PBAs on learners' achievement and teachers' practices, PBAs also have some drawbacks and limitations. One disadvantage of performance assessments is that they are relatively time and energy consuming to administer (Brown & Hudson, 1998; Colley, 2008; Crusan, 2014; Espinosa, 2015; Kirmizi & Komec, 2016; McTighe & Ferrara, 2011). In fact, the process of developing PBAs takes time since it involves different activities such as designing the performance tasks or projects, gathering materials and resources and implementing the evaluation. One reason why they can be so time consuming for teachers to evaluate is that the answers or responses to performance tasks are often less specific and require more discernment by teachers (Colley (2008). In addition, PBAs can be challenging in terms of time and labor due to the additional effort often needed for rehearsal activities or different stages of the final performance (McTighe and Ferrara, 2011).

Another reason for reluctance to use performance-based assessments may be teachers' previous experiences with them when the execution was unsuccessful or the results were inconclusive (Stiggins, 1994). This is often because teachers have not been instructed on how to implement them (Espinosa, 2015). This may lead to another issue which inhibits some teachers from implementing PBAs in their classrooms, as they worry about not knowing enough about how to fairly assess a student's performance (Airasian, 1991; Kirmizi & Komec, 2016), especially when faced with open-ended questions that can have more than one correct answer. Open-ended questions with potentially more than one answer also raise questions about the subjectivity, reliability and validity of assessment, and the impartiality, consistency and reliability of raters then become issues (Green and Hawkey, 2012). Additionally, the costs of developing performance assessments, administering them, training raters, conducting rating sessions, and reporting scores, etc., may be considerable (Brown & Hudson, 1998).

IMPLICATIONS OF PERFORMANCE-BASED ASSESSMENTS TO ENGLISH LANGUAGE CLASSROOMS

The review of performance-based assessments discussed above shows that performance-based assessments are of importance for English language teaching. Despite the problems of designing and implementing PBAs, the overwhelming body of evidence indicates that they offer many benefits over traditional standardized tests. To implement performance-based assessments in English language classroom more effectively, the following considerations should be taken into account.

First and foremost, the implementation of PBAs should be treated with the same objectivity and rigor as traditional tests because not all students' performance can be directly observable. Therefore, Brown (2004, p. 255) suggest the step-by-step guideline for the implementation of PBAs as follows:

1. Setting the overall goal of performance;
2. Specifying the detailed criteria of the performance;
3. Preparing students for performance in stepwise progressions;
4. Using a reliable evaluation form, checklist, or rating sheet,
5. Treating performances as opportunities for giving feedback and providing that feedback systematically, and
6. Utilizing self and peer-assessment judiciously.

Second, it is necessary to have rubrics for PBAs. As opposed to the traditional standardized tests, performance-based PBAs often do not have clear right or wrong answers (Brualdi, 1998). Thus, it is necessary to determine different degrees of performance achievement. In this respect, rubrics can be helpful tools to evaluate task-based forms of open-ended interactions, projects and writing (Koné, 2015), and allow teachers to determine the level of students' proficiency in performing tasks or constructing knowledge of concepts (Brualdi, 1998). Because of the crucial role of rubrics in PBAs, some major features of rubrics should also be considered to ensure the reliability of PBAs. As Brualdi (1998) mentions, designing criteria for rubrics must ensure fairness and simplicity, and these are more likely to be satisfied by well-designed analytical rubrics than holistic rubrics (Koné, 2015).

It should be stressed that the role of teachers in the process of rubric design is also crucial, and teachers need to be informed clearly of the desired outcomes before the rubrics are constructed Herrera et al., (2011). To develop reliable rubrics, teachers first need to identify what knowledge and skills will be assessed and then determine effective criteria for describing performance at different levels. Teachers also need to review the rubrics used and reflect on their assessment practices regularly, in order to determine whether their current assessment practices are consistently measuring what they are supposed to measure and whether their assessment procedures actually help their students to learn a second language more effectively (Espinosa, 2015; Sumadi, 2017). By doing this, the validity and reliability of PBAs will be addressed.

It is equally important that teachers be trained in best practices for implementing all aspects of PBAs (Chinda, 2009; Espinosa, 2015; McKay, 2006). In other words, training gives teachers the opportunity to enhance their knowledge about preparing PBA tasks (Espinosa, 2015). Teachers who are well-trained in the design and implementation of PBAs will know how to evaluate their learners' efforts and achievement during the language-learning process (McKay, 2006) and will be able link PBA evaluation criteria to learning outcomes more effectively, and, perhaps most important of all, provide them with the skills needed to make impartial, reliable assessments of the performance of language learners. Espinosa (2015) proposes five steps to help teachers develop effective PBAs, namely (1) determining what knowledge and skills are needed to assess their learners prior to developing performance tasks, (2) deciding what tasks can be used to meet the objectives of learners' outcomes, (3) creating a set of evaluation criteria which are clear to their learners, (4) analyzing learners' responses after implementing PBAs, and (5) providing learners feedback which must be descriptive and constructive.

Finally, it is crucial for raters (in most cases, active teachers) to collaborate, compare and discuss how best to carry out assessments using the same rubrics, in order to ensure consistency among assessors (O'Sullivan, 2012). This should include allowing assessor colleagues to sitting in on an assessment and then comparing assessment.

REFERENCES

Abedi, J. (2010). *Performance assessments for English language teachers.* Stanford, CA: Standford University, Standford Center for Opportunity Policy in Education.

Bass, K. M., Magone, M. E., & Glaser, R. (2002). *Informing the design of performance assessments using a content-process analysis of two NAEP science tasks.* (CSE Technical Report No. 564). Los Angeles: National Center for Research on Evaluation, Standards, and Student Testing.

Brown, H. D. (2004). *Language assessment principles and classroom practices.* White Plains, NY: Pearson Longman.

Brown, J. D. & Hudson, T. (1998). The alternatives in language assessment. *TESOL Quarterly 32,* 653-675.

Brualdi, A. (1998). Implementing performance assessment in the classroom. *Practical Assessment, Research and Evaluation 6 (2).* Retrieved from https://files.eric.ed.gov/fulltext/ED423312.pdf.

Canale, M., & Swain, M. (1980). Theoretical bases of communicative approaches to second language teaching and testing. *Applied Linguistics, 1,* 1-47. Retrieved from http://ibatefl.com/wp-content/uploads/2012/08CLT-Canale-Swain.pdf.

Chinda, B. (2009). *Professional development in language testing and assessment: A case study of supporting change in assessment practice in in-service EFL teachers in Thailand.* Unpublished PhD Thesis. The University of Nottingham, UK.

Chun, M. (2010). Taking teaching to (performance) task: Linking pedagogical and assessment practices. *Change: The Magazine of Higher Education, 42* (2), 22-29.

Colley, K. (2008). Performance-based assessment. *Science Teacher, 75*(8), 68-72.

Council of Europe. (2001). *Common European framework of reference for languages: Learning, teaching and assessment.* Cambridge: Cambridge University.

Crusan, D. (2014). Assessing writing. In A. J. Kunnan (Ed.), *The companion to language assessment,* 1, (pp. 201-215). Hoboken, NJ: Wiley-Blackwell.

Darling-Hammond, L. & Adamson, F. (2013). *Developing assessments of deeper learning: The costs and benefits of using tests that help students learn.* Standford, CA: Standford Center for Opportunity Policy in Education.

Espinosa, L. F. (2015). Effective use of performance-based assessments to identify English knowledge and skills of EFL students in Ecuador. *Theory and Practice in Language Studies 5* (12), 2441-2447.

Glisan, E., Uribe, D., & Adair-Hauck, B. (2007). Research on integrated performance assessment at the post-secondary level: Student performance across the modes of communication. *Canadian Modern Language Review, 64*(1), 39-67.

Gorp, V. K., & Deygers, B. (2014). Task-based language assessment. In A. J. Kunnan (Ed.), *The companion to language assessment, 1,* (pp. 578-593). Hoboken, NJ: Wiley-Blackwell.

Haney, W., & Madaus, G. (1989). Searching for alternatives to standardized tests: Whys, whats, and whithers. *Phi Delta Kappan*, 70, 683-687.

Herrera, S., Cabral, R., & Murry, K. (2013). *Assessment accommodations for classroom teachers of culturally and linguistically diverse students* (2nd ed.). Boston, MA: Allyn & Bacon.

Hibbard, K. M., Wagenen, L. V., Lewbel, S., Waterbury-Wyatt, S., Shaw, S., Pelletier, K., Larkins, B., Dooling, J. O., Elia, E., Palma, S. Maier, J., Johnson, D., Honan, M., Nelson, D. M., & Wislocki, J. A. (1996). *A teacher's guide to performance-based learning and assessment.* Alexandria, VA: Association for Supervision and Curriculum Development.

Kirmizi, O., & Komec, F. (2016). An investigation of performance-based assessment at high schools. *Üniversitepark Bülten, 5*(1-2), 53-65.

Koné, K. (2015). The impact of performance-based assessment on university ESL learners' motivation. *All Theses, Dissertations, and Other Capstone Projects.* 402. Available at https://cornerstone.lib.mnsu.edu/etds/402.

Krashen, S. (1981). *Second language acquisition and second language learning.* Oxford: Pergamon Press.

Lynch, B. K. (2003). *Language assessment and programme evaluation.* Edinburgh: Edinburgh University Press.

McKay, P. (2006). *Assessing young learners.* Cambridge: Cambridge University Press.

McTighe, J., & Ferrara, S. (1998). *Assessing learning in the classroom.* Washington, DC: National Education Association.

McTighe, J., & Ferrara, S. (2011). *Performance-based assessment in the classroom.* Retrieved from http://jaymctighe/wordpress/wp.context/ uploads/2011/004/performancebased-assessment-in-the-classroom.pdf.

Norris, J. M., Brown, J., Hudson, T., & Yoshioka, J. (1998). *Designing second language performance assessments.* Honolulu, US: University of Hawaii Press.

O'Malley, M., & Valdez Pierce, L. (1996). *Authentic assessment for English language learners: Practical approaches for teachers.* Reading, MA: Addison-Wesley.

O'Neil, J. (1992). Putting performance assessment to the test. *Educational Leadership, 49(8),* 14-19.

O'Sullivan, B. (2012). Assessing speaking. In C. Coombe, P. Davidson, B. O'Sullivan & S. Stoynoff (Eds.), *The Cambridge guide to second language assessment* (pp. 234-246). Cambridge: Cambridge University Press.

Pierce, L. V. (2002). Performance-based assessment: promoting achievement for language learners. *Center for Applied Linguists (ERIC/CLL News Bulletin),* 26(1), 1-3.

Stiggings, R. (2001). *Student-involved classroom assessment.* (3rd ed.). Upper Sadle River, NJ: Merril-Prentice Hall.

Stiggins, R., Arter, J., Chappuis, J., & Chappuis, S. (2007). *Classroom assessment for student learning: Doing it right—using it well.* Upper Saddle River, New Jersey: Prentice Hall.

Swain, M. (1984). Large-scale communicative language testing: A Case study. In S.J. Savignon & M.S. Berns (Eds.), *Initiatives in communicative language teaching* (pp. 185-20 1). Reading, MA: Addison-Wesley Publishing Company.

Surmadi, A. (2017). Performance-based assessment as a current trend in ELT: Investigating its washback effects on secondary-school students learning. *Kajian Linguistik dan Sastra, 2 (1).* Available at http://journals.ums.ac.id/index.php/KLS.

Volante, L. (2004). Teaching to the test: What every teacher and policy maker should know. Canadian *Journal of Administration and Policy*, 35(1), 1-6.

Watson T. R. (2006). Continuing change after the innovation. *System, (34)*, 1-14.

Wiggins, G. (1998). *Educative assessment: Designing assessments to inform and improve student performance*. San Francisco: Jossey-Bass.

Yu, G. (2014). Performance assessment in the classroom. In A. J. Kunnan (Ed.), *The Companion to language assessment, 1,* (pp. 615-630) Hoboken, NJ: Wiley Blackwell.

BIOGRAPHICAL SKETCH

Vo Phuong Quyen

Affiliation: School of Foreign Languages, Can Tho University, Vietnam

Education: Master in Education

Research and Professional Experience: teaching EAP and ESP courses, conducting research projects of related issues on internationalization in higher education, learner-centeredness, intercultural competence, and language learning strategies.

Professional Appointments: Senior lecturer

Honors: Excellent Teacher of the year 2017-2018

Publications from the Last 3 Years:

Phuong, H. Y.; Vo, P. Q., Ly, T. B. P., Luu, B. N. (2017). Factors inhibiting teachers from research engagement: A review. *Journal of Science of Can Tho University*, 6, 17-22, Available at https://sj.ctu.edu. vn/ql/docgia/tacgia-26682/baibao36183.html.

Quyen Phuong Vo (2018). Cultivating intercultural competence in a tertiary English foreign language classroom. *Developing Educational Professionals in Southeast Asia DEPISA Monograph* 5, 114-123. (ISBN 978-0-6483295-0-3).

Quyen, V. P. and Yen, P. H. (2018). English lecturers' perceptions of improving English teaching quality through action research: What do lecturers of Can Tho University say?. *Can Tho University Journal of Science*. 54(2): 98-105. DOI: 10.22144/ctu.jen.2018.013 (ISBN: 1859-2333). Available at https://sj.ctu.edu.vn/ql/docgia/tacgia-8470/baibao-38247.html.

Quyen, V. P., Nga, P. T. M. and Nguyen, H. T. (2018). Challenges to speaking skills encountered by English-majored students: A story of one Vietnamese university in the Mekong Delta. *Can Tho University Journal of Science*. 54(5): 38-44. DOI: 10.22144/ctu.jen.2018.022. Available at https://sj.ctu.edu.vn/ql/docgia/tacgia-8470/baibao-42102. html.

Vo Phuong Quyen (2018). Students' perceptions to cultivating intercultural competence activities: A case study of a Vietnamese university. *Thai TESOL Journal*, 31(1), 31-45. (ISSN 2286-8909).

Võ Phương Quyên, Đào Phong Lâm và Nguyễn Khánh Ngọc (2018). Chất lượng chương trình đào tạo cử nhân Ngôn ngữ Anh tại Trường Đại học Cần Thơ qua ý kiến của cựu sinh viên và nhà tuyển dụng. [The evaluation of English language program of Can Tho University via the voices of alumni and employers]. *Tạp chí Khoa học Trường Đại học Cần Thơ*. 54(4C): 148-158. DOI:10.22144/ctu.jvn.2018.080. Available at https://sj.ctu.edu.vn/ql/docgia/tacgia-8470/baibao-49984/doi-ctu.jsi. 2018.080.html.

Vo Phuong Quyen. (2017). Students' Experiences with English Medium Instruction (EMI) Tertiary Programs in Vietnamese Context: Implications to Curriculum Developers. The proceeding of the International Conference on "*Leadership and Management in Higher Education: Challenges, Opportunities and Ways Forward*" organized by SEAMEO RETRAC and BCCIE, Ho Chi Minh, Vietnam. Available at http://www.vnseameo.org/InternationalConference2017/materials/ 15_VoPhuongQuyen_Fullpaper.pdf.

Vo, P. Q. (2016). Promoting Mekong Delta ESL tertiary learner's speaking competence by social learning strategies. *The proceeding of the International Conference of English Language Teaching 2016: Exploring new paths to a better future of ELT in a Globalised world*, Ho Chi Minh, Vietnam, 749-812. (ISBN 978-604-73-4631-8).

Vo, P. Q. (2016). Raising intercultural competence in ELT tertiary context: What do Vietnamese English lecturers say? *The proceeding of the 2nd LITUCULI International Conference ELT Unlimited in Bangkok*, Thailand, 40-54. Available at http://www.conferences.in.th/lituculi/2016/ProceedingLITU-CULI2016.pdf.

Vo, P. Q. (2017). Rethinking Intercultural Communication Competence in English Language Teaching: A gap between lecturers' perspectives and practices in a Southeast Asian tertiary context. *I-manager's Journal on English Language Teaching*, 7 (1), 20-29 (ISSN-2231-3338). Available at https://eric.ed.gov/?id=EJ1140320.

Vo, P. Q., Ly T. B. P., Phuong, H. Y. (2016). *Improving English teaching quality using action-research: Mekong Delta teachers' perceptions*. Developing Educational Professionals in Southeast Asia (DEPISA) Thailand, Monograph 4, 60-70. (ISBN 978-0-9923846-3-0).

Vo, Q, N. Pham, N. Ho, K. Thach, H. Hoang, D. Pham. (2017). An Investigation of difficulties encountered by EFL freshmen in Speaking skill: A story from a Vietnamese tertiary context. *The proceeding of the 8th International Science, Social Sciences, Energy Conference* (I-SEEC 2017), Bangkok, Thailand, 611-617. Available at http://iseec2017.pnru.ac.th/download/Proceeding.pdf (ISBN: 978-974-316-873-4).

Yen, P. H., Phuong, L. T. B., Quyen, V. P. and Ngoc, L. B. (2018). English lecturers' perceptions and practices of research engagement: The case of Can Tho University. *Can Tho University Journal of Science*. 54(2): 122-130.DOI: 10.22144/ctu.jen.2018.016 (ISBN: 1859-2333). Available at https://sj.ctu.edu.vn/ql/docgia/tacgia-26682/baibao-38445/ doi-ctu.jsi.2018.016.html.

In: Using Alternative Assessment …   ISBN: 978-1-53615-161-9
Editors: Hoang Yen Phuong et al.   © 2019 Nova Science Publishers, Inc.

Chapter 5

IMPACT OF ONLINE PEER FEEDBACK ON STUDENTS' WRITING PERFORMANCE AND ATTITUDE

Hoang Yen Phuong and Thi Que Phuong Nguyen*

School of Foreign Languages, Can Tho University, Can Tho, Vietnam

ABSTRACT

Social media have become more and more popular all over the world, especially among adolescents. Using social media to teach English is not new and many studies have been conducted to explore the advantages that social media can bring to foreign language classrooms, especially on productive skills such as speaking or writing. Very few studies, however, have investigated one of the most popular means of social media: Facebook and its effects on students' writing skills. This study will respond to this gap by investigating whether peer feedback on Facebook can help students improve their writing performance. The current study aims to find out (1) the effects of peer feedback on Facebook on EFL students' writing performance and (2) students' attitudes towards the use of Facebook for peer feedback. This experimental study followed a one-group design using

---

* Corresponding Author's E-mail: phyen@ctu.edu.vn.

students' first drafts and final drafts of two writing topics. The study took place in one high school in Vietnam. Participants included 39 students (21 females and 18 males) of Grade 11 and four English teachers (2 females and 2 males) responsible for scoring ten model papers as well as the writing drafts. Data collected from students' writing scores and questionnaire indicated that students' writing performance increased after the study and that the majority of them had positive attitudes towards the use of Facebook for peer feedback.

Keywords: peer feedback, high school students, Facebook, writing

INTRODUCTION

With the increasing popularity of Facebook, people all over the world are using it for different purposes. Through Facebook, registered users can create profiles, upload information, send messages and photos and keep in touch with friends, family and colleagues (Dean, 2009). Although Facebook was not created for educational purposes, its functions have proved that the website can generate great potential for social learning (Pappas, 2013). In teaching and learning, Facebook has brought major benefits to both teachers and learners. For teachers, they can share course resources, fire up discussions with their colleagues, and incorporate an array of learning tools, such as videos, images, boards, chatting and private messaging (Pappas, 2013). Besides, through open groups, teachers can attract a wider audience to a specific course, domain, application or even a school. Moreover, Facebook allows teachers to receive feedback about a course or a program they are implementing, to request the audiences' opinions on a certain topic. Via Facebook, teachers can conduct questionnaires to comprehend the likes, dislikes and interests of their current students or future students and build the course around them. Facebook is also considered as a tool for teachers to upload course content, materials and resources so that colleagues can share and comment on them.

In the field of L2 writing, much research on peer feedback has been conducted via this social media platform and yielded positive results. First, students significantly improved their writing performance after they received comments from their peers and made a decision to revise the writing tasks accordingly. Second, most students found it useful to exchange feedback on Facebook and were satisfied with this type of peer review activity (Wichadee, 2013). Similar positive results were found in studies conducted by Shih (2011) and Nurlia (2014).

For teaching English in Vietnam, although the four skills of listening, speaking, reading and writing are claimed to be emphasized equally, teaching writing in high school contexts is problematic and usually brings challenges to both EFL teachers and students (Tran, 2007). Most high school students have difficulties in writing in English despite having learned English for years. Students' low level of English language proficiency, their low motivation of learning English, and the exam-driven focus are claimed to contribute to make teaching and learning L2 writing at high schools in Vietnam a challenging task.

In such a context, the current study is conducted with students at a high school in the Mekong Delta to examine whether peer feedback on Facebook can enhance EFL students' writing performance and if they have positive attitudes towards the use of Facebook for peer feedback.

LITERATURE REVIEW

Peer Feedback

Peer feedback has been defined in different ways with regard to various aspects. Most researchers emphasize the aspect of collaborative learning when defining peer feedback (Falchikov, 2001 cited in Şahin, 2008; Gennip, Segers, & Tillema, 2010 cited in Yu & Wu, 2011; Nordquist, 2014, Liu & Hansen, 2002; Teo, 2001; Topping, 2005). According to Topping (2005), peer feedback can be defined as the acquisition of knowledge and skills through active helping and supporting among learners of equal status or matched companions. It involves people from similar social groupings who are not professional teachers helping each other to learn. Peer feedback can also be viewed as a highly effective collaborative learning activity in which learners produce lesson-related artifacts, critically evaluate artifacts produced by their peers and provide them with feedback, and receive feedback from their peers regarding their own produced artifacts (Falchikov & Goldfinch, 2000; Topping, 1998; Van Gennip, Segers, & Tillema, 2010, cited in Yu & Wu, 2011). Last but not least, peer feedback is considered as a form of collaborative learning in which learners meet in small groups, either face-to-face or online, to respond to each other's Swork (Nordquist, 2014). In the current paper, peer feedback consists of all types of feedback that one student gives to others' written products via Facebook.

Peer Feedback in Learning How to Write

In teaching and learning EFL writing, a large amount of evidence has revealed the benefits of providing students with opportunities to give feedback to, and receive it from their fellow students (Liu & Carless, 2006). Peer feedback is proved to enhance students' writing performance. More specifically, peer feedback helps (1) build relationships among students, (2) develop students' communication skills, (3) develop students' critical thinking, and (4) creates opportunities for revision (Lundstrom & Baker, 2009; Tsui & Ng, 2000; Shih, 2011; Yusof et al., 2012; Scrichanyachon, 2012; Yang & Meng, 2013). In addition, peer feedback helps construct the possible collaborative relationship between writers and their readers (Charles, 1990; Tsui & Ng, 2000; Topping, 2005; Cresswell, 2000 cited in Sadeghi, 2012; Baierschmidt, 2012; Branham, 2012). According to Baierschmidt (2012), peer feedback forces negotiation with peers about the content, grammar, and rhetoric of their papers. In other words, peer feedback refers to a collaborative task during which students become better readers, and, as a result, better writers (Branham, 2012).

Moreover, peer feedback provides students with many opportunities to revise their writing drafts (Ting & Qian, 2010; Branham, 2012; Suludere, 2012; Scrichanyachon, 2012; Yusof *et al.*, 2012; Yang & Meng, 2013). With peer feedback, students can revise their products by paying attention to the comments of individuals rather than only their own (Suludere, 2012). These comments can focus on content, organization, grammar, vocabulary, mechanics, and so forth. Peer review also helps to focus the attention of authors on points they have overlooked, thereby helping them revise these points again and perhaps enhance the coherence and clarity of their texts (Suludere, 2012). Revision should result in a final draft that is much better than the first draft.

Peer Feedback in Writing a Second Language via Facebook

Various studies have investigated the use of Facebook as a means of learning English. Most of the studies were performed with university or college students in both EFL and ESL classrooms. For example, Suthiwartnarueput (2012) conducted an experimental study to investigate the effects of peer feedback via Facebook on students' grammar and writing ability. The findings indicated that the students used more correct grammatical structure and made significant improvements in writing. Experimental studies by Shih (2011), Wichadee (2013), and Nurlia (2014) explored the effects of peer feedback on students' writing performance. The results of these studies demonstrated that the students significantly improved their writing ability and had positive attitudes towards the use of peer feedback on Facebook. However, although Facebook is now popular among Vietnamese youth, no studies have attempted to investigate the effects of using Facebook as a means to learn English writing.

THE STUDY

Research Questions

The current research was conducted to find out the answers to two research questions:

1) What are the effects of peer feedback on Facebook on Vietnamese high school students' writing performance?
2) What are their attitudes towards the use Facebook for peer feedback?

Participants

The participants include 39 eleventh graders (21 males and 18 females) and 5 teachers of a high school in Vietnam. These students were assumed to be at low-intermediate level of English language proficiency based on their English final results in the previous school year and the results of the test at the beginning of the school year 2014-2015. Many of them had low motivation in learning English. They had very few opportunities to be exposed to English outside the classroom and they learned English just because it was a subject in the school curriculum.

The participants also included a teacher researcher and four other EFL high school teachers of English. The teacher researcher was responsible for teaching the writing topics and instructing the students on how to give peer feedback on Facebook. Four highly-experienced teachers including two females and two males were also invited to participate in the study and were responsible for scoring students' texts.

Research Instruments

The research instruments of the study include the first drafts and final drafts of the two writing topics: (1) Write a description of a popular festival in Vietnam, and (2) Write a description of a city or a place in Vietnam you would like to visit. These two topics were selected from the topics the students learn from their course books.

An analytic grading scale adapted from Reid (1993) was chosen for scoring the writing drafts with the following proportions: topic sentence:

10%; content: 20%; organization: 20%; vocabulary use: 15%; grammar: 15%; use of transitions: 10%; and conclusion: 10%.

The participants were asked to evaluate their own attitudes about using peer feedback on Facebook by choosing the extent to which they agreed with each item of a 30-item 5-point Likert scale questionnaire. The questionnaire consists of 30 items categorized into three main clusters: (1) Facebook as a means for peer feedback and learning English, (2) skills and knowledge the students gained from peer feedback on Facebook, and (3) difficulties the students encountered in the process of peer feedback on Facebook.

Research Procedure

The study was conducted over a period of 12 weeks. In the first week, one of the researchers introduced the research project to students and all students agreed to participate voluntarily in the project. All these voluntary students already had a Facebook account and made friends with each other on this social media platform. Then, the students were asked to form groups on Facebook. After groups were established, the students were given instructions on how to write comments and how to give peer feedback via Facebook. The final activity of this week was that both the teacher and students worked together reading a model paragraph and wrote sample comments on that piece of writing. In Week 2, the first topic was taught to the students.

After the lesson, students were required to write the first draft and then post it on Facebook. In week 3, 4 and 5, they were responsible for exchanging feedback on Facebook based on the teacher's guidelines for each feedback (see Table 1).

Week 6 was the time for giving and receiving the final feedback on topic 1 and the students were asked to write the final draft on this topic and post on Facebook. A hard copy of the final draft was also sent to the teacher. The same procedure was repeated for the second topic over a period of 5 weeks, from Week 6 to Week 11. The last week - Week 12 - was the time for the researcher to collect the questionnaire and conduct the interviews.

**Table 1. Turns and guidelines for peer feedback
for the one group of four**

Feedback	Turns	Guidelines
1	student 1 → student 2 student 2 → student 3 student 3 → student 4 student 4 → student 1	1. Is the text easy to understand? Do you enjoy the text? 2. What parts of the text do you find particularly interesting?
2	student 1 → student 3 student 2 → student 4 student 3 → student 1 student 4 → student 2	3. Are there main ideas and supporting ideas in the text? 4. Is the information organized in a clear and logical way? 5. Are there any transitions? What are they? Are they used in a good way?
3	student 1 → student 4 student 2 → student 1 student 3 → student 2 student 4 → student 3	6. Are there any parts that seemed unclear or confusing to you? What are they? 7. Are there any errors in vocabulary, grammar, spelling, and verb tenses? What are they? How can you correct them?
4	student 1 → student 4 student 2 → student 3 student 3 → student 1 student 4 → student 2	8. Is there any information that needs to be expanded or added? 9. What should be done to improve the text?

FINDINGS

The Effects of Facebook on Students' Writing Performance

The results of the data analysis show that the mean score of the final draft (M_{final} = 6.70, SD_{final} = 1.74) was higher than that of the first draft (M_{first} = 6.44, SD_{first} = 1.67). A General Linear Model (GLM) Test for repeated measures conducted on the mean scores of the first draft and the final draft of the first showed that there was a significant difference between these two drafts (F =19.52, df = 38, $p < .01$. It can therefore be concluded that the writing performance of students in the first topic increased significantly.

Besides, the scoring components of the first draft and the final draft of the first topic (topic sentence, content, organization, vocabulary, grammar, transition, and concluding sentence) were also put into comparison and analysis. A Descriptive Statistics Test was run on the mean scores of the components of the first draft and final draft of this topic. The results of these components were presented in Table 2.

In terms of individual rating categories, mean scores for content (F = 7.02, df = 38, $p = 0.01$), vocabulary (F = 8.52, df = 38, $p < 0.01$) and transition (F = 6.22, df = 38, $p = 0.01$) were significantly better for the final draft compared to the first draft. However, there was no statistical difference in mean scores between first and final drafts for topic sentence (F = 1.00, df = 38, $p = 0.32$), organization (F = 2.05, df = 38, $p = 0.16$), grammar (F = 2.91, df = 38, $p = .10$), or concluding sentence (F = 1.00, df = 38, $p = .32$).

Similar trends between first and final drafts were obtained for the second topic, with a significantly higher (F = 9.65, df = 38, $p < .01$).overall mean for the final draft ($M_{final} = 7.41$, $SD_{final} = 1.81$) compared to the first draft ($M_{first} = 7.18$, $SD_{first} = 1.88$).

**Table 2. Writing components of the first draft
and the final draft of the first topic**

Component	Number	First draft		Final draft	
		Mean	Standard Deviation	Mean	Standard Deviation
Topic sentence	39	.89	.27	.87	.27
Content	39	1.30	.42	1.4	.45
Organization	39	1.38	.39	1.40	.39
Vocabulary	39	.96	.31	1.03	.33
Grammar	39	.81	.26	.85	.27
Transition	39	.32	.32	.37	.35
Concluding sentence	39	.81	.26	.82	.28

Likewise, trends in scores for individual components between first and final drafts of the second assignment (Table 3) were generally similar to those observed in the first assignment (Table 2). Mean scores increased from the first to final draft in all components, except the topic sentence. However, the improvement was only significant for two components, content (F =

10.32, df = 38, $p < 0.01$) and vocabulary (F = 4.96, df = 38, $p = 0.03$); there was no significant difference in mean scores for the topic sentence (F = 2.05, df = 38, $p = 0.16$), organization (F = 3.83, df = 38, $p = 0.06$), grammar (F = 3.16, df = 38, $p = 0.08$), transitions (F = 2.79, df = 38, $p = 0.10$) or concluding sentence (F = 1.40, df = 38, $p = 0.24$) between first and final drafts in the second assignment. Thus, while there was some evidence for an improvement in performance from the first to the final draft in most categories they were only significant in terms of content and vocabulary.

There was a clear and highly significant (F = 19.05, df = 38, $p < 0.01$) improvement in mean score from the first draft of the first assignment ($M_{1st\text{-}draft}$ = 6.44, $SD_{1st\text{-}draft}$ =1.67) to the final draft of the second assignment ($M_{final\text{-}draft}$ = 7.41, $SD_{final\text{-}draft}$ = 1.81). This indicates a general improvement in writing performance during the study.

**Table 3. Writing components of the first draft
and the final draft of the second topic**

Component	Number	First draft		Final draft	
		Mean	Standard Deviation	Mean	Standard Deviation
Topic sentence	39	.83	.25	.81	.31
Content	39	1.46	.43	1.56	.38
Organization	39	1.44	.42	1.47	.42
Vocabulary	39	1.06	.29	1.10	.31
Grammar	39	.97	.24	.99	.25
Transition	39	.63	.43	.65	.41
Concluding sentence	39	.79	.33	.83	.32

The findings of the current study are in line with those by Mangelsdorf (1992), Shih (2011), Suthiwartnarueput and Wasanasomsithi (2012), Wichadee (2013), and Nurlia (2014) that using online tools as a means of giving feedback helps EFL students to improve their writing skills. For example, in Wichadee's (2013) study, scores of the final drafts were statistically higher than those of the first drafts, and the first draft average score in the second writing was higher than that in the first writing. It is consistent with Suthiwartnarueputa and Wasanasomsithi's (2012) study in one point and inconsistent with the same study in another point. The common finding of the two studies is that students significantly developed their writing performance during the study. The difference between the two studies is that in Suthiwartnarueput and Wasanasomsithi's (2012) study, students' use of grammatical structures improved significantly, while in the current study, students did not make improvement in using grammatical structures. This could result from the fact that students in the current study had reached a good grammar level that little or no improvement could be made.

In addition, the finding of the present study is both consistent and inconsistent with Mangelsdorf's (1992) study. The two studies share the same result, that is, most of the students made progress in the content of their writing works. However, in Mangelsdorf's (1992) study, students' works were improved in terms of organization while in the current study students' writing performance did not develop in this aspect. This can be because students had learned how to write a paragraph with good organization before. Therefore, there was little space for improvement.

Students' Attitudes towards the Use of Facebook for Peer Feedback

Facebook as a Good Means for Peer Feedback and Learning English

Based on a 5-point Likert scale, a majority of students (mean = 3.96, SD = 0.54) agreed that using Facebook provided a good medium for peer feedback and learning English. A value of 4 on a 5-point Likert scale is considered relatively high, and the mean of 3.96 above is not statistically different from 4 in a one-sample T-test (t = -0.42, df = 38, p = 0.67). This suggests that students have a positive attitude to the use of Facebook as a mechanism for peer feedback and learning English, and there was broad consensus that using Facebook provided a good opportunity to read a wide range of writing and share opinions on it.

Skills and Knowledge Students Gained from Peer Feedback
on Facebook

The data analysis result revealed that student' perception in this aspect was slightly high (M= 3.77, SD = .73). A One-Sample T-Test was run on the mean score of participants' attitudes towards the skills and knowledge they gained from peer feedback on Facebook (M = 3.77, SD = .73) and the test value was 4, which is assumed to be relatively high in a five-point scale. The results showed that the mean score of participants' agreement was not statistically different from 4 (t = -1.92, df = 38, p = .06). Therefore, it can be concluded that the students had relatively positive attitudes towards the skills and knowledge they gained from peer feedback on Facebook. Among the skills and knowledge they gained, the highest mean fell into the attitudes towards the revision which made their writing products better (M = 4.10, SD = 1.02).

Difficulties the Students Encountered in the Process of Peer Feedback
on Facebook

The students' attitudes towards the difficulties they encountered in the process of peer feedback on Facebook was above average (M= 3.41, SD = .56). A One-Sample T-Test was conducted on the mean score of participants' attitudes towards the difficulties they encountered in the process of peer feedback on Facebook (M = 3.41, SD = .56) and the test value of 4, which is considered high in a five-point scale. The result shows that the mean score of participants' attitudes towards the difficulties was different from 4 (t = -6.39, df = 38, p = .00). Therefore, it can be concluded that the degree of difficulties they encountered in the process of peer feedback on Facebook was high. Among the difficulties they faced, the biggest difficulty fell into the transference of the ideas from their first language to the target language in the process of writing (M = 3.97, SD = .87). Another difficulty was the quality of peer feedback (M = 3.92, SD = .66) because they sometimes did not understand what their friends meant in their feedback.

The findings from the current study are consistent with the findings from studies by Suludere (2012), who considers that peer feedback helps students to revise the content, organization, grammar, vocabulary, and mechanics of the text as well as the points that they have not noticed before and add them to the coherence and comprehension of their texts.

Students also experienced some difficulties in the process of writing peer feedback on Facebook. The most challenging problem they faced was the transference of ideas from their mother tongue to the target language, a common tendency of most EFL learners. This caused difficulties and affected the quality of writing because the target language is significantly different from their native language. This finding is similar to the study by Muhammed & Ameen (2014) in that idea transference from L1 to L2 is considered to be a major problem for EFL learners. The idea is also in line with Ellis (1997 cited in Muhammed & Ameen, 2014) and Thuy (2009), who argue that one of the factors that affects the quality of L2 writing is interference from the first language. In fact, in the process of writing in a foreign or second language, L2 /FL students usually transfer from L1 to L2, especially the idea transfer (Muhammed & Ameen, 2014).

Furthermore, in the current study, the students also faced problems with the quality of peer feedback. Some of the feedback was less useful and too difficult to understand. The main reason for this could be lack of linguistic competence which includes vocabulary and grammar. As a result, some of the students could not revise their writing drafts and the scores of the final drafts stayed the same as those of the first drafts, and issue also described by Mojica (2010 cited in Hammad, 2014), Ahmed (2010) and Watcharapunyawong and Usaha (2013). The findings from the study conducted by Mojica (2010) revealed that vocabulary and grammar are perceived by EFL students to be the most difficult aspects of writing.

CONCLUSION AND IMPLICATIONS

The research results reported in this study indicate that the high school students made significant improvement in their writing performance and had positive attitudes towards the use of Facebook for peer feedback. Despite its small sample size, this study demonstrates that using Facebook as a means of peer feedback offers promising opportunities for language teaching in Vietnamese high schools. However, this kind of research should be replicated with a larger population and a wider range of high schools in Vietnam to verify its broader relevance in language teaching in the Vietnamese context.

REFERENCES

Ahmed, A. H. (2010). Students' problems with cohesion and coherence in EFL essay writing in Egypt: Different perspectives. *Literacy Information and Computer Education Journal*, 1(4), 211-221.

Baierschmidt, J. (2012). Japanese ESL learner attitudes towards peer feedback. *The Journal of Kanda University of International Studies*, 24, 101-114.

Branham, C. A. (2012). *Electronic peer feedback in a collaborative classroom*. Unpublished Graduate Theses and Dissertations. Retrieved May 20, 2018 from http://scholarcommons.usf.edu/cgi/viewcontent.cgi?article=5183&context=etd.

Dean, A. (2009). *Definition Facebook: Part of the Internet technologies glossary*. Retrieved June 5, 2018 from http://whatis.techtarget.com/definition/Facebook.

Falchikov, N., & Goldfinch, J. (2000). Student peer assessment in higher education: A meta-analysis comparing peer and teacher marks. *Review of Educational Research*, 70(3), 287-322.

Hammad, E. A. (2014). Palestinian university students' problems with EFL essay writing in an instructional setting. *Journal of Second and Multiple Language Acquisition*-JSMULA, 2(1).

Liu, J., & Hansen, J. G. (2002). *Peer Response in Second Language Writing Classrooms*. Ann Arbor: University of Michigan Press.

Liu, N. F., & Carless, D. (2006). Peer feedback: the learning element of peer assessment. *Teaching in Higher education*, 11(3), 279-290.

Lundstrom, K., & Baker, W. (2009). To give is better than to receive: The benefits of peer review to the reviewer's own writing. *Journal of Second Language Writing*, 18(1), 30–43.

Mangelsdorf, K. (1992). Peer reviews in the ESL composition classroom: What do the students think? *ELT Journal*, 46(3), 274-284.

Muhammed, A. A., & Ameen, C. A. M. (2014). Idea transformation between L1 and L2 as a writing problem for Kurd EFL learners at different University levels. *International Journal of Scientific & Engineering Research*, 5(7).

Nordquist, R. (2014). *What are the characteristics of good writing?* Retrieved September 18, 2017 from http://grammar.about.com/od/tz/g/writingterm.htm.

Norman, L. (2012). *Analytical versus holistic marking schemes.* Retrieved January 30, 2018 from https://teachingformiles.wordpress.com/2012/04/07/analytical-versus-holisticmarking-schemes/.

Nurlia, R. (2014). *The Effectiveness of Online Peer Feedback through ClosedGroup Facebook on the Students of Writing Achievement.* Unpublished S2 Thesis. Malang: State University of Malan.

Pappas, C. (2013). *How to use Facebook for social learning.* Retrieved January 12, 2018 from http://elearningindustry.com/how-to-use-facebook-for-social-learning.

Reid, J. M. (1993). *Teaching ESL Writing.* Englewood Cliffs, NJ: Regents.

Sadeghi, K., & Baneh, M. D. (2012). Relationship between student self-monitoring, type of peer feedback and EFL writing performance. *Theory and Practice in Language Studies*, 2(5), 909-915.

Şahin, S. (2008). An application of peer assessment in higher education. *The Turkish Online Journal of Educational Technology*, 7 (2).

Shih, R. C. (2011). Can Web 2.0 technology assist college students in learning English writing? Integrating Facebook and peer assessment with blended learning. *Australian Journal of Educational Technology*, 27(5), 829-845.

Srichanyachon, N. (2012). An investigation of university EFL students' attitudes toward peer and teacher feedback. *Educational Research & Review*, 7(26), 558-562.

Suludere, H. N. (2012). *Online peer feedback and learner autonomy in English as a foreign language writing classes.* Unpublished master thesis - Universita Ca Foscari Venezia, Italy.

Suthiwartnarueput, T., & Wasanasomsithi, P. (2012). Effects of using Facebook as a medium for discussions of English grammar and writing of low-intermediate EFL students. *Electronic Journal of Foreign Language Teaching, 9*(2), 194-214.

Teo, A. K. (2001). *Using a peer assisted writing activity to promote ESL/EFL students' narrative writing skills.* Unpublished thesis. Chung Shan Medical University, Taiwan.

Thuy, N. H. H. (2009). Teaching EFL writing in Vietnam: Problems and solutions - a discussion from the outlook of applied linguistics. *VNU Journal of Science, Foreign Languages*, 25, 61-66.

Ting, M. E. I., & Qian, Y. U. A. N. (2010). A case study of peer feedback in a Chinese EFL writing classroom. *Chinese Journal of Applied Linguistics*, 33(4), 87-98.

Topping, K. J. (2005). Trends in Peer Learning. *Educational Psychology*, 25(6), 631– 645. University of Dundee, Scotland.

Tran, L. T. (2007). Learners' motivation and identity in the Vietnamese EFL writing classroom. *English Teaching: Practice and Critique*, 6(1), 151-163.

Tsui, A. B., & Ng, M. (2000). Do secondary L2 writers benefit from peer comments? *Journal of Second Language Writing*, 9 (2), 147-170.

Watcharapunyawong, S., & Usaha, S. (2012). Thai EFL students' writing errors in different text types: The interference of the first language. *English Language Teaching*, 6(1), p67.

Wichadee, S. (2013). Peer feedback on Facebook: the use of social networking websites to develop writing ability of undergraduate students. *Turkish Online Journal of Distance Education (TOJDE)*, 14(4).

Yang, Y. F., & Meng, W. T. (2013). The effects of online feedback on students' text revision. *Language Learning & Technology*, 17(2), 220–238.

Yu, F. Y., & Wu, C. P. (2013). Predictive effects of online peer feedback types on performance quality. *Educational Technology & Society*, 16 (1), 332–341.

Yusof, J., Ab Manan, N. A., & Alias, A. A. (2012). Guided peer feedback on academic writing tasks using Facebook notes: An exploratory study. *Procedia-Social and Behavioral Sciences*, 67, 216-228.

BIOGRAPHICAL SKETCHES

Hoang Yen Phuong

Affiliation: School of Foreign Languages, Can Tho University

Education: Ph.D. Language and Education

Research and Professional Experience: learning autonomy, teaching writing, self-regulated learning, testing and assessment, task-based language teaching

Professional Appointments: Senior Lecturer, Vice Dean

Thi Que Phuong Nguyen

Affiliation: Tam Vu 3 High School

Education: MA English Teacher Education

Research and Professional Experience: teaching writing

Professional Appointments: Teacher

In: Using Alternative Assessment ...   ISBN: 978-1-53615-161-9
Editors: Hoang Yen Phuong et al.   © 2019 Nova Science Publishers, Inc.

Chapter 6

BENEFITS AND CHALLENGES OF USING ANALYTIC RUBRICS FOR STUDENTS' SPEAKING SELF-ASSESSMENT

Hoang Yen Phuong[*] *and Thanh Xuan Phan*
Can Tho University, Can Tho, Vietnam

ABSTRACT

English teachers usually encounter problems when assessing students' speaking skills in big classes of forty students or more. They do not have enough time to give feedback to each individual student in speaking lessons, which prevents students from recognizing their speaking errors and improving their skills. A rubric, which makes assessment quick and efficient, is a promising way to solve this problem. Not only does a rubric help teachers in their assessment, but students can benefit greatly from it as well. Speaking rubrics, however, have not yet been researched from students' perspectives. This study was therefore conducted over a period of 15 weeks in a high school English class in Vietnam to explore: (1) students' perceptions towards the benefits of using an analytic rubric for their self-assessment, (2) some problems they encountered when they use the rubric to assess themselves. The study involved 98 students from a high school in Can Tho city. The research follows a descriptive approach with a twenty-five item questionnaire using a five-point Likert scale. The results reveal that students had various benefits and problems of using analytic rubrics for their self-assessment of speaking skills.

Keywords: formative assessment, speaking performance, analytic rubrics

INTRODUCTION

All kinds of assessments conducted by teachers or learners have two functions (Boud, 2003). The first is to develop knowledge and appreciate appropriate standards and criteria; second is to make a judgment about the work involved to see whether it is good or not.

There are many ways to make assessments but self-assessment, the subject of this paper, is a method that has not been widely used for assessing students. It is a key element in formative assessment because it involves students in reflecting on their own work based on stated goals or criteria, rather than depending too much on the teacher's role in assessment. Self-assessment by students is done on drafts of work in progress to revise and improve the final product.

The assessment of speaking involves a number of procedures and it is usually an extremely difficult task for teachers. Self-assessment of their own speaking by students can lighten the work of teachers and, from a student perspective, can also promote learning and help develop higher-order skills such as self-reflection and critical thinking. However, oversize classes in Vietnam make it challenging for both students and teachers to assess speaking performance within the limited time given for classroom activities.

Rubrics offer a promising solution to many of the challenges of speaking assessment because they provide a set of scoring guidelines for evaluating students' work. To provide reliable and unbiased scoring, a rubric should contain a clear description and scoring guidelines for each criterions. It can be assigned by numbers - the higher the number, the better the performance. Wiggins (1991), who advocates the use of explicit criteria to enable students to assess themselves, asserted that the development of self-assessment is an inherent part of any assessment aimed at improving learning. It is for this reason that rubrics form the backbone of assessment based on outcomes (Popham, 1997; Holmes & Smith, 2003; Andrade & Du, 2005), and that students should be encouraged to take responsibility for their own learning through self-assessment which, in turn, would provide students with the opportunity to develop meta-cognitive and more general learning skills (Hendry, 1996).

Studies of students' responses to the use of rubrics show that graduate and undergraduate students value rubrics because they clarify targets for their work, allow them to regulate their progress, and make grades or marks more meaningful and fair. However, few studies have explored the impact of rubrics, especially analytical rubrics, on students' speaking performance as well as their perceptions toward this assessment tool. The current study was conducted to fill such gaps. The two research questions posed in the current study are:

1. What are students' perceptions toward the benefits of analytic rubrics in assessing their own speaking performance?
2. What challenges do students encounter when implementing analytic rubrics in assessing their own speaking performance?

LITERATURE REVIEW

Rubrics

In student assessment, a rubric is a set of scoring guidelines for evaluating students' work. Nitko (1996) defined a scoring rubric as a coherent set of rules in order to assess the quality of a student's performance. It can be in a form of a rating scale or a checklist.

A common definition of a rubric used by several researchers is that a rubric is a document presenting the expected outcomes for a certain work evaluated by listing the criteria and followed by the scale of quality (from excellent to poor) (Reddy & Andrade, 2010). To provide reliable and unbiased scoring, a rubric needs a clear description of expectations for each criterion, and scoring strategies that use a scale to interpret how well a candidate performs in each criterion. It can be assigned by numbers - the higher the number, the better the performance (Wiggins, 1998).

There are two common types of rubrics, namely holistic and analytic. Both are used to assess student products and performances (Wiggins & McTighe, 2005). A holistic rubric is used to assess different levels of overall performance. It gives a single score or rating for a product or performance. An analytic rubric, on the other hand, breaks up a product or performance into discrete categories and judges each separately. Consequently, a separate score is provided for each category and those scores are then combined to give an ovall assessment of the quality of the response (Linn & Gronlund, 2000; Wiggins & McTighe, 2005). Thus, an analytic rubric gives students more detailed feedback on specific areas of the assignment. An effective analytical rubric requires a careful design with clearly identified criteria and levels of performance that students must display to demonstrate proficiency (Truemper, 2004; Suskie, 2009; Spence, 2010).

Benefits of Rubrics

Research has shown that using rubrics for assessment provides five clear benefits - fairness and objectivity - more effective tracking of student progress - influences teaching positively - gives better feedback to both students and teachers - fosters student thinking and learning.

Firstly, according to Stergar (2005), at the beginning of a project, students should be given a rubric with clear criteria. Then students would know what is expected and that the teacher's grading is fair and consistent. Thus, one of the main benefits of using a rubric with specific scoring criteria is the objectivity it brings to the rating of student performance.

Second, traditional assessment procedures focusing mainly on numeric or letter grades make it hard for teachers to track students' progress and help them with specific ongoing problems. On the other hand, rubrics provide teachers with a tool that allows them and their students to identify strengths and weaknesses, and to form a detailed record of track progress more easily. Teachers can take a quick look at several rubrics to find information on areas where a student's work is good or bad (Stevens & Levi, 2005). Rubrics also help educators know whether learners are making progress by setting up a baseline of a student's ability in each of the four strands of language: speaking, listening, writing and reading (Murphy, 2009). Using separate rubrics for each strand allows documentation of proficiency levels in specific strands and helps teachers to choose the next steps for instruction in a specific strand.

Third, rubric-based assessments can have a positive impact on teaching because they help to identify specific weaknesses in language use, thereby encouraging teachers to review and adapt their teaching practices to address those deficiencies (Dunbar, Brooks & Kubichka-Miller (2006). This allows teachers to modify their teaching mode between instructing, facilitating, tutoring or mentoring, depending on the objectives and needs of their students.

Teachers are also more likely to sustain focus on assessment criteria throughout instruction when they set the criteria before the test, thus helping them to stay focused on the process of learning and their objectives in the course (Stergar, 2005). In addition, teachers can use rubrics to conduct student conferences and set goals for the next learning step, thereby encouraging mastery of their current skillset, and either confirming a job 'well-done' or designing corrective measures.

The fourth area in which rubrics provide clear benefits is student feedback. Effective feedback to students requires extensive description of the perfect level of achievement (Steven and Levi, 2005). As a matter of fact, rubrics fulfill this demand well. They offer students more useful feedback about strengths and weaknesses than traditional forms of assessment do not (Andrade, 2000). Students need more than a single score, they may not find out their mistakes and how to improve their performance for the next assignment (Moskal, 2000). In addition, well-written instructional rubrics can provide clearness and equity and assist students in better understanding how teachers score their papers as rubrics provide performance expectations with various criteria (Andrade, 2000).

Last but not least, rubrics are claimed to promote students' thinking and learning. The use rubrics by students to assess their own work and that of their classmates means that they are taking responsibility for their own learning through self-assessment. This provides them with the opportunity to develop metacognitive and more general learning skills (Hendry, 1996). The rubric format helps students to draw their own conclusions about strengths and weaknesses in their work, and this self-discovery is one of the positive outcomes from using rubrics, because it encourages them to think critically about their own learning. Used in conjunction with good academic advice, rubrics can play a key role in helping students develop a more scholarly form of critical thinking.

Before assigning the task, it is better to discuss the rubric with the students, in order to promote critical thinking (Steven and Levi, 2005). A successful collaborative effort in the development and design of rubrics with second and third grade students was reported by Skillings and Ferrel (2000), who found that students were able to perceive the rubric critically and generate the elements of the rubrics by themselves after receiving some instruction on the use of rubrics. Being involved in designing rubrics, looking for suitable criteria and participating in serious self- and peer assessment has a powerful impact on student learning (Andrade, 2000). A study by Cohen, Lotan, Scarloss, Schultz, and Abram (2002) has shown that students who were informed of the evaluation criteria for written essays and were encouraged to self-assess their work, had higher-quality discussions and better group products than students who worked without knowing the criteria.

Challenges of Using Rubrics

While well-designed rubrics make the assessment process more valid and reliable, their real value lies in advancing the teaching and learning process. However, having a rubric does not necessarily mean that the evaluation task is simple. The best rubrics allow evaluators and teachers to draw on their professional knowledge and to use that professional knowledge to rate performance without bias.

One of the drawbacks of rubrics is that creating a good, well-designed rubric takes a long time and, for this reason some authors argue that they should only be developed for complex assignments, especially in writing (Gezee et al., 2012). There is also a risk that a poorly designed rubric, especially one that is too broad or too narrow, will hinder learning because it is not believed by students (Reddy and Andrade, 2010). This makes it a challenge for both teachers and students to design a well-balanced and reliable rubric.

Notwithstanding what appears to be clear benefits from using rubrics for assessment, there still seems to be some debate over whether students should be allowed to use them for self-assessment and peer assessment, with some arguing for not allowing their use by students (Kohn, 2006), and others supporting their use by students on the grounds of honesty and respect for students (Andrade, 2006).

In short, using rubrics in the EFL classroom has both benefits and challenges. Despite the extensive literature on the application of rubrics in teaching writing, few studies have been conducted to explore student perceptions of using analytic rubrics for self-assessment of their speaking skills. The current study was an attempt to fill such a gap.

THE STUDY

Participants

Ninety-eight students, including 69 females and 29 males in a high school for the gifted in Vietnam were invited to participate in this study. The participants consisted of students studying the Pilot English Program at Grade 10 and who had already experienced the use of analytic rubrics before. This pilot program was implemented with new text books and trained teachers, and it aims to improve the English language skills of Vietnamese students compared to the traditionally used textbooks published decades ago.

These students were recruited to be the subjects of the study for three reasons. First, they had been studying with the Pilot English Textbook since grade 6, which meant that they had all experienced the new teaching methods and accumulated a lot of English language knowledge and skills. Second, they all had good basic skills in English and their average scores were quite good. Lastly, they had all been introduced to and used analytic rubrics in their studies in the first semester of Grade 10. Therefore, their perceptions towards the use of analytic rubrics are likely to be more accurate and practical.

The Questionnaire

A questionnaire of 25 items was employed to explore students' perceptions toward the use of analytic rubric for students' self-assessment in speaking. The questionnaire was partly adapted from the survey by Haugnes and Russell (2014). The items of the questionnaire were grouped into 4 clusters as listed in Table 1 below.

Each item in the questionnaire follows a five-point Likert Scale, where participants indicated the extent to which they agreed or disagreed with the statements (1 – strongly disagree, 2 – disagree, 3 – neutral, 4 – agree, and 5 – strongly agree). This instrument was chosen because of its simplification and high reliability.

Table 1. Cluster of the questionnaire items

Cluster	Items
General benefits of rubrics	3, 5, 8, 15, 20, 22, 21, 25
Benefits of an analytic rubric to students' preparation of a presentation	1, 2, 10, 14, 19
Benefits of an analytic rubric to students' evaluation of their own work	6, 11, 12, 13, 16, 18, 24
Students' difficulties in using rubrics	4, 9, 17, 23

Research Procedure

The questionnaire was first tested with 40 students, who were asked to answer a pilot questionnaire written in Vietnamese. A Cronbach's alpha of 0.64 was gained, which is quite acceptable (Gliem, 2003). As a result of students' answers and feedback on the pilot questionnaire and their suggestions for its improvement, some adjustments were made to the final questionnaire given to all students.

The finalized questionnaire was administered to 98 students over a period of two weeks. To ensure reliable data, students were given careful instructions before completing the questionnaire, including information on the purpose of the study, and they were asked to be honest and serious in responding the items. Participants were allowed 10-15 minutes to complete the questionnaire.

FINDINGS AND DISCUSSION

Students' Perception toward the General Benefits of Analytic Rubrics for Self-Assessment

Regarding students' perceptions toward the general benefits of analytic rubrics in self-assessment, most of the items in the first cluster received positive feedback from the students (see Table 2). More specifically, two thirds of the participants agreed that a rubric enables them to know the course expectations and helps them to self-assess their skill and presentation performance. Moreover, 76.6% of the participants believed that the rubric made the evaluation fair and meaningful. In addition, 72.4% of students agreed that it was easier for them to comprehend a teacher's grading if he or she evaluated the presentation based on the rubrics. Moreover, 70.4% of participants agreed that rubrics helped them improve their oral presentation performance.

Other benefits that students claimed to receive from the implementation of analytic rubric could be found with Item 22, Item 25 and Item 20. For example, more than sixty-five percent of students believed that they learnt much more when they used rubrics in class. Rubrics with detailed criteria helped students to find out the standard to which they would try to follow. With the rubrics, they looked for more information and learned more so as to reach the objective, therefore, they could enhance their learning. Moreover, students could compare their marks with their friends easily with the use of rubric, with 58.2% of agreement. Consequently, students claimed that they were less surprised with their marks since they used the rubric.

Table 2. Students' perceptions towards the general benefit of an analytic rubric in self-assessment

Item	Agree (%)	Disagree (%)	Neutral (%)
Item 8: It enables me to know the course expectations and self-assess my skill and presentation performance.	77.5	4.1	18.4
Item 5: The rubrics made evaluation fair and meaningful.	76.6	2	21.4
Item 15: It is easier for me to understand my teacher's grading if he or she would evaluate my presentation basing on the rubrics.	72.4	3.1	24.5
Item 8: It improves my oral presentation performance.	70.4	2	27.6
Item 22: I learn much more if I use rubrics in class.	65.3	5.1	29.6
Item 25: Rubrics help me to compare my mark with that of other students easily.	58.2	8.1	33.7
Item 20: I am less surprised with my grade since I use the rubric	54.1	8.1	37.9
Item 3: I like the use of rubrics because it enables me to know what is expected of me.	46.9	8.2	44.9
Item 21: I have fewer questions about my assignment when I use rubric.	35.7	20.4	43.9

However, students disagreed most (43.9%) with Item 21 which says "*I have fewer questions about my assignment when I use rubric.*" In other words, students thought they still had many questions to ask about their assignment when they used a rubric. This could be because students were not very familiar with the use of a rubric and thus they had questions about applying it to assess their performance.

In general, students' positive perceptions of students toward the use of rubrics were consistent with what Stergar (2005) found in his study. Therefore, EFL teachers may consider applying analytic rubrics in their speaking classroom, especially when they want to evaluate students' oral presentation performance.

Students' Perception toward the Benefits of Analytic Rubrics in Self-Evaluating Their Preparation for Oral Presentation

With regard to the benefits of analytic rubrics in students' self-evaluation of their preparation for oral presentation, it can be seen from Table 3 that the students are well-aware of the benefits that analytic rubrics bring them in the process of preparing their oral presentation. Most noticeably, 86.6% of participants think that a rubric is a good tool to show them what the teacher wants them to do with the presentation. They can use the rubric to check their work beforehand and it can help them stick to the topic (Item 14 and Item 19, with 76.5% and 75.5% of agreement respectively).

Furthermore, students agreed that they could check their preparation basing on rubrics beforehand (71.4%) and feel it easy to prepare their oral presentation (62.3%).

In short, the results showed that most students have a positive attitude towards the use of analytic rubrics for their preparation of a presentation. The evidence from this section further supports the benefits of using rubrics for oral presentation skills. This is in line with the benefits of Andrade's (2000) and Cohen et al. (2002).

Table 3. Students' perceptions towards the benefit of analytic rubrics to students' preparation of a presentation

Item	Agree (%)	Disagree (%)	No idea (%)
Item 2: It shows me what the teacher wants me to do with the presentation.	86.8	2	11.2
Item 1: The rubric helps me stick to the topic.	76.5	4.1	19.4
Item 10: It enables me to understand the objective of the task.	75.5	5.1	19.4
Item 14: I can check my oral preparation basing on the rubrics beforehand	71.4	4.1	24.5
Item 19: I feel easy to prepare my presentation because I use the rubric to stick to my topic.	62.3	9.1	28.6

Students' Perception toward the Benefits of Analytic Rubrics in Evaluating Their Own Oral Presentation

Table 4 shows students' perception toward the benefits of analytic rubric in evaluating their own oral presentation.

One benefit of rubrics is to provide detailed feedback, which are about students' strengths and weaknesses with 83.7% of agreement. More than three fourth of participants agreed with the facts that rubrics enable them to assess themselves and makes it easier for evaluation (with 76.5% and 75.5% respectively).

For Item 18 *"I still need my teacher's explanation after using the rubric."* 71.4% of the students agreed. These figures suggest that students think the role of teacher feedback in evaluation is still very important, even when students use a rubric for self-evaluation.

The two items that received the most disagreement from the participants are Item 24 and Item 16. In other words, students did not think that rubrics could completely replace the role of teacher' feedback as well as their further explanations.

**Table 4. Students' perceptions towards the benefit
of analytic rubrics to evaluate their own presentation**

Item	Agree (%)	Disagree (%)	Neutral (%)
Item 6: Rubrics give me detailed feedback of my strengths and weaknesses.	83.7	5.1	11.2
Item 11: It enables me to assess myself.	76.5	3.1	20.4
Item 12: The rubric makes it easier for evaluation.	75.5	4.1	20.4
Item 18: I still need my teacher's explanation after using the rubric.	71.4	9.2	19.4
Item 13: I can assess myself after I present my topic.	70.4	6.1	23.5
Item 16: I don't need any further explanations from my teacher after using the rubric to assess myself.	9.2	64.3	26.5
Item 24: If rubrics are used, there is no need for feedback from the teacher.	9.2	78.6	12.2

In general, the results in this cluster showed that the students are well-aware of the benefits a rubric brings them in the process of evaluating their own presentation but also recognize the role of the teacher in helping them improve their oral performance via his or her feedback and explanations. The finding in this section is in accordance with suggestions by Steven and Levi (2005) about involving both teachers and students in the process of rubric implementation.

Students' Perceptions toward the Challenges of Using Analytic Rubrics for Their Speaking Self-Assessment

The last cluster of the questionnaire reveals the students' perception towards the difficulties of using analytic rubrics for their speaking self-assessment.

**Table 5. Students' perceptions towards the difficulties
of using analytic rubrics for their speaking self-assessment**

Item	Agree (%)	Disagree (%)	Neutral (%)
Item 23: I think the rubric is difficult for me because my English level is too low.	58.2	9.1	32.7
Item 5: I am afraid of making something new out of the rubrics.	24.5	46.9	28.6
Item 12: Rubrics hinder my creativity.	15.4	53	31.6
Item 24: The rubric is too complicated for me to use because it has lots of information.	10.2	50	39.8

The biggest challenge for students seems to be that they do not have sufficient English skills to use rubrics easily and effectively. For the other three items, a very small percentage of students agreed that rubrics might cause these problems. This is inconsistent with the challenges that Reddy & Andrade (2010) proposed. In their study, rubrics hindered students' creativity. Most students in the current study, however, did not think that an analytic rubric hindered their creativity.

CONCLUSION

The research has focused on the students' perceptions toward the use of analytic rubric for their self-assessment of speaking performance. The findings in the study imply that rubrics can be considered as a useful instructional and assessment tool in helping students to assess their own speaking skills. Most of the findings are consistent with what has been found in the literature review. Through the findings and the results, it may be concluded that students have positive perceptions of the benefits of analytic rubrics in both the process of preparation and the evaluation of their own presentation.

REFERENCES

Andrade, H., and Du, H. (2005). Student perspectives on rubric-referenced assessment. *Practical Assessment, Research & Evaluation, 10*(5), 1-11.

Andrade, H. G. (2000). Using rubrics to promote thinking and learning. *Educational leadership, 57*(5), 13-19.

Bolton, C. F. (2006). Rubrics and adult learners: Andragogy and assessment. *Assessment Update, 18*(3), 5–6.

Boud, D. (2003). *Enhancing learning through self-assessment.* London: Routledge.

Dunbar, N. E., Brooks, C. F., & Kubichka-Miller, T. (2006). Oral communication skills in higher education: Using a performance-based evaluation rubric to assess communication skills. *Innovative Higher Education, 31*(2), 115-127.

Gezie, A., Khaja, K., Chang, V. N., Adamek, M. E., & Johnsen, M. B. (2012). Rubrics as a tool for learning and assessment: What do baccalaureate students think? *Journal of Teaching in Social Work, 32*(4), 421-437.

Gilmore, B. (2007). Off the grid: The debate over rubrics-and what it's missing. *California English, 13*(1), 22-25.

Hendry, G. D. (1996). Constructivism and educational practice. *Australian Journal of Education, 40*(1), 19-45.

Holmes, L. E., & Smith, L. J. (2003). Student evaluations of faculty grading methods. *Journal of Education for Business, 78*(6), 318-323.

Jonsson, A., & Svingby, G. (2007). The use of scoring rubrics: Reliability, validity and educational consequences. *Educational research review, 2*(2), 130-144.

Kohn, A. (2006). The trouble with rubrics. *The English Journal, 95*(4), 12–15.

Linn, R. L., & Gronlund, N. E. (2000). *Measurement and assessment in teaching.* Upper Saddle River, New Jersey: Prentice-Hall.

Moskal, B. (2000). Scoring rubrics: What, when and how? *Practical Assessment,Research & Evaluation, 7*(3). Retrieved from http://pare online.net/getvn.asp?v=7&n=3.

Murphy, A. F. (2009). Tracking the progress of English language learners. *Phi Delta Kappan, 91*(3), 25-31.

Nitko, Anthony J (1996). *Educational assessment of students* (2nd ed). Upper Saddle River, N.J.: Merrill.

Popham, W. J. (1997). What's Wrong – and What's Right – with Rubrics. *Educational Leadership, 55*(2), 72-75.

Powell, T. A. (2001). *Improving assessment and evaluation methods in film and television production courses.* PhD dissertation, Capella University. UMI No. 3034481.

Quinlan, A. M. (2006). A complete guide to rubrics: Assessment made easy for teachers, K-College. USA: Rowman & Littlefield Education. Reddy, Y. M., & Andrade, H. (2010). A review of rubric use in higher education. *Assessment & evaluation in higher education, 35*(4), 435-448.

Reddy, Y. M., & Andrade, H. (2010). A review of rubric use in higher education. *Assessment & evaluation in higher education, 35*(4), 435-448.

Schneider, J. F. (2006). Rubrics for teacher education in community college. *The Community College Enterprise 12*(1) 39–55.

Skillings, M. J., & Ferrell, R. (2000). Student-generated rubrics: Bringing students into the assessment process. *The Reading Teacher, 53*(6), 452-455.

Spence, L. K. (2010). Discerning writing assessment: Insights into an analytical rubric. *Language Arts, 87*(5), 337.

Stergar, C. (2005). *Performance tasks, checklists, and rubrics.* Glenview: Pearson Education.

Stevens, D. D., & Levi, A. J. (2005). *Introduction to rubrics: An assessment tool to save grading time, convey effective feedback, and promote student learning.* Virginia: Stylus Publishing.

Suskie, L. (2009). Using assessment results to inform teaching practice and promote lasting learning. In *Assessment, Learning and Judgement in Higher Education* (pp. 1-20). Springer, Dordrecht.

Truemper, C. M. (2004). Using scoring rubrics to facilitate assessment and evaluation of graduate-level nursing students. *Journal of Nursing Education, 43*(12), 562-564.

Turley, E. D., & Gallagher, C. W. (2008). On the uses of rubrics: Reframing the great rubric debate. *The English Journal, 97*(4), 87-92.

Wiggins, G. (1991). Standards, Not Standardization: Evoking Quality Student Work. *Educational Leadership, 48*(5), 18-25.

Wiggins, G. (1998). *Educative Assessment. Designing Assessments To Inform and Improve Student Performance.* Jossey-Bass Publishers, 350 Sansome Street, San Francisco, CA 94104.

Wiggins, G., & McTighe, J. (2005). *Understanding by design (2nd ed.).* Alexandria, VA: Association for Supervision and Curriculum Development ASCD.

BIOGRAPHICAL SKETCHES

Thanh Xuan Phan

Affiliation: Chau Van Liem High School

Education: MA English Teacher Education

Research and Professional Experience: teaching speaking

Professional Appointments: Teacher

In: Using Alternative Assessment …   ISBN: 978-1-53615-161-9
Editors: Hoang Yen Phuong et al.   © 2019 Nova Science Publishers, Inc.

Chapter 7

THE IMPLEMENTATION OF PORTFOLIOS IN ACADEMIC WRITING CLASSROOM

Thi Thu Nga Phan[*]

Faculty of Foreign Languages, Ho Chi Minh City Open University,
Ho Chí Minh City, Vietnam

ABSTRACT

The presented study aims at investigating if using portfolios as a continuous assessment tool could help students develop their autonomy, which was examined in their willingness and ability to work independently after class. Twenty-three students in their second year of the academic writing course at the faculty of foreign languages in Ho Chi Minh City Open University took part in this study. Students' independent learning activities include choosing the topic for writing their essays, searching for relevant resources, making an informal outline, making a detailed outline with source information, writing the first draft, peer and self-editing, and writing final draft. This writing course lasted in 12 weeks, and students had to submit their final products in the final class meeting. Students' learning outcomes were continuously assessed from choosing the topic to writing a complete essay. The questionnaire with three main parts: independence of

[*] Corresponding Author's E-mail: nga.ptt@ou.edu.vn.

learning, study habits and skills needed for self-studying was used to collect data after students fulfilled their writing course. The analysis of the collected data reveals that with the portfolio assessment, students could develop their responsibility, motivation, and self-confidence which contribute to the willingness to work independently of autonomous learners though there are some differences between the paper-based portfolio and E-portfolio groups. Some limitations of the study and recommended further studies on the portfolio assessment can be found at the end of this chapter.

Keywords: portfolio assessment, the paper-based portfolio, E-portfolio, independent learning

INTRODUCTION

How to assess students' independent learning has become one of the major concerns of the instructors of English in universities since the Ministry of Education and Training of Vietnam issued Decree 43 in 2007, which requested the application of the credit-based training system in all universities. Because one of the most important requirements of this training system is encouraging students to study independently, many researchers as well as lecturers in universities in Vietnam are still worrying about the problems of this training system such as how to manage students' independent learning and how to assess their learning outcome after class. Like many other universities in Vietnam, Ho Chi Minh City Open University (HCMCOU) applied the credit-based training system since the academic year 2009-2010; however, there have not been many studies on how to assess students' independent learning activities in this university. The findings of Phan (2014) indicated that 90% of participants did not spend enough time on their independent learning activities as requested in the syllabus of the course English Language Teaching Methodology. Phan (2015) concluded that the instructor's use of the paper-based portfolio in the class of testing and assessment methods was very effective in developing student-teachers' willingness to work independently, which could be seen in their responsibility, self-confidence and motivation. In another study conducted by Phan and others (2017), there are some differences in the findings from students' self-assessment and that of the instructors' observation. The results from participants' responses indicated that working with E-portfolios on Google Sites had positive effects on their responsibility and motivation, but these participants did not highly self-assess their self-confidence when studying independently. However, the analysis of the instructors' observation and records revealed that 67% of participants were highly motivated when working independently; 34% of these were motivated and responsible for their learning; and 43% less positive in both motivation and responsibility. In another study conducted by Phan (2018), the findings showed that when working with E-portfolios on Google Sites, student-teachers could develop their motivation and responsibility, which are among important personal qualities of autonomous learners; and their self-assessing skill, one of the most important skills that autonomous learners need. In addition, there is significant correlation between student-teachers' willingness and ability to work independently when comparing their responsibility, motivation and self-confidence with various skills such as creating E-portfolios, writing English tests, choosing materials, reading, planning time for doing tasks, managing studying time, monitoring their studying, self-assessing and reflecting. In all of the above studies, both the paper-based portfolio and E-portfolios used as a continuous assessment tool to evaluate students' learning process after class were examined in classes of student-teachers, and the results of students' learning process occupied only 40% of the learning outcome of the whole course. In fact, there have not been many studies on the portfolio assessment in English writing classes in HCMCOU in particular and in other universities in Vietnam in general. As a result, the author wished to investigate if the portfolio assessment could help students develop their autonomy in an academic writing class, and students' autonomy was examined both in their willingness and ability to work independently.

REVIEW OF RELEVANT LITERATURE

Definitions of Portfolio and E-Portfolio

There are many different definitions of portfolios. Paulson, Paulson and Meyer (1991) define: "A portfolio is a purposeful collection of student work that exhibits student's effort, progress and achievements in one or more areas. The collection must include student participation in selecting contents, the criteria for selection, the criteria for judging merit, and evidence of student self-reflection" (Paulson et al., 1991, p.60). In addition, according to Spratt, Pulverness and Williams (2011), a portfolio is a collection of learners' work done over a course or a year which shows evidence of development of their language skills. Usually, portfolios let learners produce work on an area just after it has been taught (Spratt et al., 2011, p. 147).

According to Barrett (2005), there are two basic types of portfolios based on the purposes of usage: assessment and learning portfolios. On the one hand, in assessment portfolios, students present their products, assignments or tasks to meet the requirements of a course or a program. On the other hand, learning portfolios are collections of work and artefacts assembled by the learners to show their learning process; therefore, the focus of this type of portfolios is to enhance learning and demonstrate the development of the learner over time.

E-portfolio or electronic portfolio, as defined by Lorenzo and Ittelson (2005), is the personal and digital collection of artefacts of an individual including 'demonstrations, resources, and accomplishments' for a variety of contexts and time periods, and this collection can be comprised of text-based, graphic, or multimedia elements archived on a Web site or on other electronic media such as a CD-ROM or DVD. Today, the E-portfolio involves the situation of a portfolio within a web- based interface, and the use of a web-based interface makes the portfolio process more flexible and dynamic and allows individuals to contribute to and alternate their *E-portfolios* in a way that is immediately accessible to employers or instructors. The word *artefacts* in an E-portfolio can indicate text-based work, reflections, video demonstrations, and other multimedia elements such as blogs and wikis that are included in the *E-portfolio* to both promote and demonstrate learning (Brandes and Boskic, 2008).

Although E-portfolios can be created on various platforms, Schaefer (2016) believes that Google Sites is a great application for creating E-portfolios because of its great advantages. One of the most remarkable advantages of this kind of E-portfolio can be seen in its great privacy controls. Thanks to Google, a user can easily make his/her personal site private, share it with selected individuals or make it entirely public and open to the world. Another advantage is that Google Sites provides a lot of useful features; i.e., it is free, has no ads, and is customizable. Because it is a Google product, it works smoothly with Google Docs, YouTube, Google Calendar, Picasa web albums. Moreover, a portfolio created on Google Sites is never married to a school's servers, so long after a student is no longer affiliated with a school, s/he can keep updating and accessing his/her portfolio, without worrying about eventually being pushed out to make way for current faculty and students. Finally, like many other Google products, Google Sites is very simple to edit and maintain. If a user wants his/her own domain name, s/he can purchase it and have it redirect to his/her Google Sites (Schaefer, 2016). Therefore, with such benefits of Google Sites, students can create E-portfolios of their personal, professional and academic work. They can also collaborate with other students around the world to share ideas, create content and communicate ideas. Students can assemble, present, and share information online for documenting academic growth, career evaluation, and course preparation. Finally, they can maintain and expand individual E- portfolios over the duration of a class and beyond university years.

Benefits and Challenges of Using the E-Portfolio as an Assessment Tool

Several benefits associated with portfolios are claimed by many researchers such as Brown (2004), Barrett (2005), Tosh, Light, Fleming and Haywood (2005) and Wetzel and Strudler (2006), Spratt and others (2011).

These authors believe that portfolios can help students improve technology knowledge and skills, facilitate distribution, store many professional documents, and increase accessibility. Brown (2004) believes that portfolios can effectively be used in writing and reading classes. Lorenzo and Ittelson (2005) claim that with E-portfolios, students may not only showcase the best work as a professional, but also exhibit their knowledge and skills in using technology. Moreover, E-portfolios can serve as an administrative tool to manage and organize work created with different applications and to control who can see the work; E-portfolios also encourage personal reflection and often involve the exchange of ideas and feedback (Lorenzo and Ittelson, 2005). Also, portfolios can be used both for assessment by the teacher and for students' self-assessment. In general, portfolio is a type of formative and continuous assessment with a number of advantages because it is inclusive, informative, developmental, reflective and easy to integrate into teaching and learning (Spratt et al., 2011, pp. 147-148).

Despite many benefits mentioned above, portfolios may challenge both the lecturers and students. Brown (2004) believed that if used as an assessment tool, the practicality of portfolios could be lower than that of other forms of assessment because of three reasons such as time constraints for both the instructor and students, costs and administrative details. Moreover, as cited in Wray (2007), according to many authors like Pecheone et al. (2005); Wetzel and Strudler (2005) and Wilhelm et al. (2006), the primary and most obvious barrier to the successful integration of E-portfolios into a teacher education program is the technology. Also, as indicated in Wray (2007), navigating the technology challenges of uploading files and digital images and linking to online sources can be a daunting and frustrating task for student-teachers with weak technology background. The same challenge can be seen for the teacher trainer who is responsible for writing the criteria to evaluate the final products and for reviewing and assessing student-teachers' completed tasks on E-portfolios. Besides challenges of providing training and support, according to Wray (2007), not all students have access to the type of technology and peripherals like scanners, video cameras, and audio recording equipment that they need to create E-portfolios at home. Moreover, perhaps the biggest concern with E-portfolios is about the time and attention needed to ensure a successful experience for both the lecturer and student-teachers where training program goals and purposes as well as students need are met (Wray, 2007). In addition to technology challenges, other problems such as the lack of self-assessment, reflection, and metacognitive skills in students' educational background may decrease the effectiveness of E-portfolios (Yastibas and Cepik, 2015). The last challenge may come from inexperienced teachers who implement E-portfolios in their courses, and their lack of experience with the E-portfolio process can cause problems for the implementation of the system. Implementation of E-portfolios requires learning how to use the software for the E-portfolio platform and understanding the assumption on which an E-portfolio is built (Yastibas and Cepik, 2015).

Definitions of Autonomy and Autonomous Learners

Autonomy

There are many well-known definitions of autonomy according to different authors. As cited in Benson (2006), Holec (1981), the father of learner autonomy, states that autonomy is 'the ability to take charge of' (Benson 2006, p. 22). Dickinson (1987) defines autonomy as 'a situation in which the learner is totally responsible for all the decisions concerned with his [or her] learning and the implementation of those decisions' (Benson, 2006, p.22). Little (1991) proposes that autonomy is 'essentially a matter of the learner's psychological relation to the process and content of learning (Benson, 2006, p.23). In addition, Benson (2006) argues that autonomy is a recognition of the rights of learners within educational systems. Moreover, Thornbury (2006) believes that autonomy is one's capacity to take responsibility for and control of his/her own learning in either an institutional context or completely independent of a teacher or institution; it is also called *self-directed learning* (2006, p. 22). Furthermore, Peréz Cavana (2012) cited another definition of self-directed learning from Knowles (1975, p.18) as follows:

In its broadest meaning, self-directed learning describes a process in which individuals take the initiative, with or without the help of others, in diagnosing their learning needs, formulating learning goals, identifying human and material resources for learning, choosing and implementing appropriate learning strategies, and evaluating learning outcomes.

Autonomous Learners

William (1997) argues that autonomous learners possess both willingness and ability to act independently. Particularly, learners' willingness to work independently depends on the level of their motivation and confidence; also their level of knowledge and skills positively affect their ability to act independently (William, 1997, p. 82). Moore (2008) suggests that conceptualizing learner autonomy involves two factors: (i) an autonomous learner has developed the capacity to take at least some control over their learning; and (ii) the learning environment provides opportunities for learners to take control of their learning. To develop this capacity, autonomous learners are required to have a set of personal qualities like confidence, motivation, taking and accepting responsibility and ability to take initiative; and this capacity also involves a set of skills: academic, intellectual, personal and interpersonal. Macaskill and Taylor (2010) believe that elements of responsibility for learning, openness to experience, and intrinsic motivation with an element of self-confidence in tackling new activities are core components of autonomous learning or independence of learning.

Stages of Autonomous Learning

Reinders and Balcikanli (2011) recommended that to study successfully, autonomous learners should spend eight stages such as identifying learning needs, setting goals, planning learning, selecting resources or materials, selecting learning strategies, learning (practice), monitoring progress, assessment and revision. All of these stages form a cycle, and they always impact learners' reflection, motivation and interaction with the language and other learners. One of the stages of the autonomous learning cycle is planning learning, and it can be supposed that effective learners should know how to organize their learning, which is line with Moore's view (2008). That is, autonomous learners can organize their learning to prove their responsibility for their own learning. In addition, Macaskill and Taylor (2010) argue that autonomous learners should own good learning habits including effective time management and positive attitudes towards lone working. Also, autonomous learners must be able to self- assess their learning outcome in order to reflect their ability to choose materials as well as learning methods, to plan and to monitor their learning process.

Levels of Autonomous Learning

Figure 1. The cycle of the interactive self-directed learning process. Reinders and Balcikanli (2011, p. 20).

Nunan (1997) defines five levels of autonomous learning including awareness, involvement, intervention, creation and transcendence. At the awareness level, learners are made aware of the pedagogical goals and content of the materials they are using, and they identify strategy implications of pedagogical tasks and identify their own preferred learning styles/strategies. At the involvement level, learners are involved in selecting their own goals from a range of alternatives on offer. Particularly, they make choice among a range of options. At the intervention level, learners are involved in modifying and adapting the goals and content of the learning program; that is, they modify and/or adapt tasks. At the creation level, learners create their own goals and objectives, which means that they create their own tasks. At the transcendence level, learners go beyond the classroom and make links between the content of the classroom learning and the world beyond so that they can become teachers and researchers (Nunan, 1997, p. 195).

Portfolios and Learner's Autonomy

In comparison with some traditional methods of assessment such as class progress tests and achievement tests, there are some advantages of using portfolios as a tool in developing learner autonomy (Richards and Renandya, 2002; Brown, 2004; Spratt et al., 2011). Many authors such as William (1997), Moore (2008), Macaskill and Taylor (2010), Reinders and Balcikanli (2011) pointed out the relations between portfolios and learner's autonomy. One of the most remarkable advantages is that portfolios offer students opportunities to evaluate their work, and this kind of assessment emphasizes students' participation in the evaluation process; and students are also requested to be responsible for their learning and evaluating. Therefore, the process of working with portfolios helps learners to develop self-assessing skill, an important skill of an autonomous learner, as well as to become responsible for their own learning, and responsibility is also among important personal qualities of an autonomous learner. Another important feature of using portfolios as an assessment tool is that learners take active control of their learning process by using metacognitive strategies such as planning, organizing, monitoring, observing and reflecting, and the use of these strategies can enhance learners' autonomy. Finally, portfolios emphasize learners' participation, so they have opportunities to reflect on their performance, show their learning process and progress, and to present the results of their learning; therefore, they will have a sense of achievement, which motivates them to continue their autonomous learning, and motivation is among personal qualities of an autonomous learner.

Previous Relevant Research Findings

Tosh, Light, Fleming, and Haywood (2005) believed that motivation, assessment and E-portfolio technology are major emerging themes that need to be addressed to make using an E-portfolio a more rewarding experiencing for many students. The results of their study show that an institution or more specifically a course, needs to identify the learning outcome of using E-portfolios and ensure that the E-portfolios are aligned with the rest of the course. Next, the results of Wetzel and Strudler (2006) identified many benefits of E-portfolios such as increasing opportunities for students to reflect and learn, helping students to understand teaching standards and increasing faculty communication with students. Despite some existing disadvantages, these authors concluded that faculty satisfaction with E-portfolios appeared strongly associated with their values for student-centered in teacher education and in some cases, their willingness to sacrifice individual preferences to accomplish program goals. Next, according to Kocoglu's conclusion (2008), E-portfolios have been potential tools for enhancing reflective thinking and professional development of student-teachers. The findings of another author, Young (2008) prove that the use of E-portfolios promotes a greater impetus for the student to assume a personal responsibility for his/her own development, in the process of taking of individual control over his/her progression towards becoming a teacher. Therefore, the student-teacher is provided with the opportunity for constant reflection rather than the periodic reflection offered by traditional paper-based portfolios. Then Akçil and Arap (2009) concluded that students had positive attitudes towards using the E-portfolio for educational purposes because it provided them permanent learning and gave them the possibility of controlling themselves and increased their motivation to study. After that, Smolyaninova (2010)'s conclusions prove that E-portfolios help student-teachers improve self-evaluation skills, form critical view on the personal achievement, and raise level of profession ambition. The results of Caner (2010) indicated that the subjects in this study generally preferred to be evaluated by traditional paper and pencil tests, and a number of subjects had negative attitudes towards portfolio assessment in their writing courses. However, most of these subjects believed that portfolio assessment could contribute to their English learning processes.

Nezakatgoo (2011) concluded that students whose work was evaluated by a portfolio system had improved their writing, and gained higher scores in final examination in comparison with students whose work was evaluated by the traditional evaluation system. Nzakatgoo (2011) also suggested that portfolio assessment could be used as a complementary alternative along with traditional assessment to shed new light on the process of writing. The findings of Taki and Heidari (2011) indicated that portfolio-based writing assessment had a positive effect on language learning and writing ability. Hung (2012) notes that E-portfolio assessments generate positive washback effects on learning such as building a community of practice, facilitating peer learning, enhancing learning of content knowledge, promoting professional development and cultivating critical thinking. In spite of such benefits, the E-portfolio assessment brings some negative washback effects like learning anxiety deriving from larger audiences, and resistance to technology.

The findings of the study conducted by Cakir and Balcikanli (2012) indicated that both student- teachers and teacher-trainers found the use of E-portfolios beneficial in terms of reflection, self- assessment and awareness. Furthermore, Douglas (2012) found that *E-portfolios* were effective in developing self-directed learning skills. Particularly, E-portfolios had positive effects on students' intrinsic motivation, self-assessment, self-confidence and self-esteem. Also, the findings of Kaliban and Khan (2012) indicate that the student-teachers in their study appreciated E-portfolios as their performance and achievements were traced over time. They also found that E-portfolios which function as a monitoring tool could help these student- teachers recognize their learning and identify their strengths and weaknesses. However, there were some challenges such as validity and reliability, interrupted Internet connection, negative attitudes of the participants, time constraints, workload and ethical issues. In terms of teacher competencies, they identified six competencies that emerged from the student-teachers' practices of E-portfolios: (i) developing understanding of an effective teacher's role; (ii) developing teaching approaches/activities; (ii) improving linguistic abilities; (iv) comprehending content knowledge; (v) gaining information and communication technology skills; and (vi) the realization of the need to change mindsets.

Fahim and Jalili (2013) indicated both advantages and drawbacks of using the portfolio assessment. The participants in Fahim and Jalili (2013)'s study agreed that this assessment method allowed them to decide on what they liked to write. Moreover, by working with portfolio, these participants became aware of their strength and weakness, and this way of assessment provided the teacher with insights on adjusting relevant feedback to the students' needs. However, the majority of students believed that using the portfolio assessment was a frustrating and time consuming task. In spite of such limitations, these authors concluded that the portfolio assessment outweighed the traditional way of testing, so it enabled students to use editing successfully and improved their writing proficiency.

Aygün and Aydin (2016), on the one hand, conclude that E-portfolios develop reflective learning, writing skills and increase motivation; on the other hand, they reveal that E-portfolios have some limitations and adverse effects such as learning anxiety, students' resistance to technology. The findings of the study conducted by Obeiah and Bataineh (2016) revealed that the portfolio group outperformed the conventionally-instructed group in their overall writing performance and in their performance on the writing subskills of focus, development, organization, conventions and word choice. The results of Ucar and Yazidi (2016) showed that students had positive attitudes towards using portfolios on improving their writing skills in ESP classes. The findings of Vangah, Jafarpour, and Mohammadi (2016) indicated that while the portfolio assessment group and the traditional assessment group were homogeneous in terms of their writing proficiency before the treatment phase, the portfolio group outperformed the traditional assessment group in the post-writing test. These authors claim that portfolio assessment has a significant positive effect on EFL learners' overall writing ability and that portfolio assessment can also offer authentic information about the progress of the students, and can be used as a means of helping them overcome their writing anxiety in foreign and second language learning.

In brief, as reviewed in literature, many researchers appreciate the use of portfolios as an assessment tool to help students of English develop their autonomy, although both the instructors and students have to deal with some challenges. The results from relevant studies conducted by researchers have also approved the effectiveness of the portfolio assessment in English language education; however, as stated from the beginning of this article, there have not been many studies on the use of portfolios as an assessment tool in English language education in Vietnam. From such theoretical base and empirical findings; therefore, it is supposed if portfolios are successfully used as an assessment tool, the instructors will be able to monitor and assess students' independent learning after class, which can contribute to the effectiveness of the credit-based training system in not only HCMCOU but also other universities in Viet Nam. In the next part of this article, an investigation on the use of portfolios in an academic writing class in HCMCOU and the findings of this study will be presented.

RESEARCH METHOD

The purpose of the conducted study aims at finding the answer to the following question:

> Could the use of the paper-based portfolio and E-portfolio as a continuous assessment tool help the second year students in an academic writing class develop their autonomy, in terms of their willingness and ability to study independently?

Setting and Participants

There are 34 students majoring in English in their second year at the beginning of the Academic Writing Course; however, only 23 students fulfilled this course and took part in answering the questionnaire after they finished their final work, and 11 students did not finish their final essays, so these students did not participate in this study. Among 23 students, 16 students volunteered to create E-portfolios on Google Sites and eight students used paper-based portfolios to display their writing tasks during the course. This writing course lasted in 12 weeks from January 11th, 2018 to April 27th, 2018. There were no class meetings during traditional Tet holidays (from February 5th, 2018 to March 5th, 2018). The students attended class once a week.

This academic writing course equips students the skills necessary to write coherent, and logical university-level essays. There are four units in the textbook – Academic Writing Skills 3 (Chin et al., 2015), and each covers an important element of successful academic writing. By the end of the course, in term of knowledge students are expected to be able to list important elements of a university-level essay including understanding essay prompts, describing effective paragraphs from the introduction to the conclusion and choosing sources used in the essay. In term of academic writing skills, students will be able to interpret essay prompts, do research, develop ideas in essay paragraphs, search, evaluate, and cite sources according to APA style, use hedging and intensifying and write academic sentence styles. In term of attitudes, students will be able to collaborate with their peers, meet the deadlines for writing tasks and avoid plagiarism when writing their essays. At the end of the course, students had to submit two essays. They worked in groups of three or four to write essay about 500 words (40% out of 100% of the learning outcome of the whole course), and each individual had to write an essay about 700 words (60%). The detailed schedule of the academic writing class can be seen below.

Table 1. Detailed schedule of the academic writing class

Week	In class activities	Self-studying activities
1	- Unit 1: Preparing to write - Understanding the essay prompts - Taking a position - Doing research - Planning the essay	- Choosing the topics for group essays - Searching for relevant sources
2	- Unit 2: Essay paragraphs - Introductory paragraphs - Body paragraphs - Logical fallacies - Concluding paragraphs	- Making informal outlines
3	- Unit 3: Using and citing sources - Evaluating sources - Integrating source information - Citing sources - Using reporting verbs and phrases	- Evaluating sources - Making detailed outlines - Adding details to the outlines using paraphrased, summarized and quoted sources
4	- Unit 4: Accuracy and clarity - Hedging and intensifying - Academic sentence styles - Editing	- Writing the first draft - Peer editing - Choosing the topic and sources for the individual essay
5	- Submitting the group essay - Checking individual topics and sources	- Modiying sources and writing an informal outline
6	- Peer feedback on the outline of the individual essay	- Writing a detailed outline - Using paraphrases, summaries, and quotations in the outline
7	- Peer feedback on the detailed outline	- Improving the detailed outline - Writing the first draft
8	- Peer feedback (focusing on the APA style) on the first draft	- Improving the first draft after getting peer feedback
9	- Self checking and peer feedback on accuracy and clarity	- Editing language accuracy and clarity
10	- The lecturer's feedback on each individual essay	- Editing and writing the final draft
11	- No class meeting	- Editing and writing the final draft
12	- Submitting the individual essay	- Answering the questionnaire

Contents of Students' Portfolios and Criteria to Evaluate Their Tasks

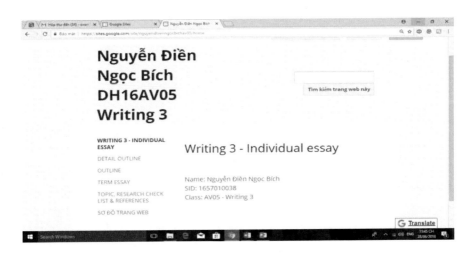

Figure 2. One example of an E-portfolio.

As presented above, students had to write two essays: one done in group of three or four and the other individually. For the group essay, the students' paper-based portfolios include: (i) a cover page with students 'personal information such as their full names and students' ID numbers; (ii) a checklist of witting tasks they did in groups like the topic of their essay, a list of resources used in their essays and evaluation sheets of these resources, a formal outline, a detailed outline with quotations, summaries and paraphrases, the first draft of their essay and the second draft or complete essay with the reference list; (iii) and writing tasks including peer feedback and the instructor's feedback which are chronologically put in a plastic folder. These students' traditional portfolios were checked by the instructor in class once a week. The students' E-portfolios on Google Sites consist the main page with their personal information, and subpages covering writing tasks like those in the paper-based portfolio group. Whenever these students completed one of their writing tasks, they invited the instructor as well as their classmates to visit their E-portfolios to have feedback. The instructor usually had feedback on these students' work at home and if they had any problems, they could ask the instructor for further explanation in class.

Similarly, the students did the same things and followed the same procedures as they did in their group essays when they wrote their individual essays. The interface or the main page an E-portfolio created by one of the students looks like in Figure 2.

Criteria to Evaluate Students' Work in Their Portfolios

The students' essays written in a group were examined in many aspects. They would be awarded one mark for a well-stated thesis statement and for an introduction that is interesting and relevant to the topic. If all of the main ideas and supporting details in the body paragraphs are clearly stated and closely related, they would be awarded one mark for the unity of ideas in their essay. Then another mark would be awarded for the coherence of the essay. That means the paragraphs and sentences in paragraphs follow one another in the logical way of the kind of the essay and transitions are used to connect ideas within a paragraph and to link paragraphs in the essay. In addition, students were awarded four marks for the supporting ideas in their essay. These ideas were examined in terms of the sources of information, the methods to integrate source information such as paraphrases, summaries and quotations, and the citation of sources according to the APA style. The other three marks were awarded for students' ability to use language accurately and appropriately; especially their ability to use sophisticated language and conventions of writing academic essays.

Students' individual essays were also checked and assessed many times. The results of students' completed essays would be based on their writing process (50%) and their final essays (50%). For writing individual essays, students spent many writing tasks such as choosing the topic and making a list of references using the APA style (5%), writing an informal outline (10%), writing a detailed outline including integrating sources in three different methods (25%), and peer and self-editing twice: once for checking the effectiveness of the essay, and the other for checking mechanics (10%). Students' final individual essays were marked in terms of the essay format according to the APA style (20%), coherence and unity (10%), and language

(20%); especially students' ability to use hedging, intensifying and academic sentence styles were examined.

Instrument and Data Collection

The instrument used to collect the data was the questionnaire consisting of two main parts. The first part of this questionnaire is a 12 item measure with two subscales measuring Independence of Learning (Items from 1 to 7), and study habits (from items 8 to 12). Seven items were labeled as students' independence of learning or willingness to work independently including motivation, openness, self-confidence and responsibility; and five items were labeled as study habits such as managing time, planning, meeting deadlines, procrastination and attitude toward lone working. This measure is called autonomous learning scale which was developed by Macaskill and Taylor (2010). The second part of the questionnaire consists of 10 items labelled as skills like creating E-portfolio, academic writing, reading, collaborating, selecting materials, choosing learning strategies, planning their study, self-assessing, monitoring and reflecting that students needed when they studied independently after class. The students in two groups gave responses to the same questionnaire. However, the second part of the questionnaire for the students in the paper-based portfolio includes nine items (without creating E-portfolio skill). Students' responses for items from 1 to 12 were recorded on a 5-point scale with higher scores indicating greater levels of autonomy, more independence and more positive attitude towards autonomous learning. However, item 11 (*I frequently find excuses for not getting down to work*) is negatively worded to help prevent response bias in participants. Therefore, the lower score for this item is, the student's better habit becomes. From items 13 to 22, students were asked to self-assess their ability to work independently or skills they used during their writing course in five different levels: (5) extreme success, (4) success, (3) OK, (2) failure and (1) extreme failure. The questionnaire was sent to students' emails after they submitted their final essay and they were asked to send their responses back to the lecture one week later.

FINDINGS

Findings from the Paper-Based Portfolio Group

Table 2. Autonomous learning of the paper-based group

	N	Minimum	Maximum	Mean		Std. Deviation
	Statistic	Statistic	Statistic	Statistic	Std. Error	Statistic
Responsibility	8	3,00	5,00	4,6250	,26305	,74402
Self-confidence (1)	8	3,00	5,00	4,2500	,25000	,70711
Motivation (2)	8	3,00	5,00	4,0000	,32733	,92582
Openness (1)	8	3,00	5,00	3,7500	,25000	,70711
Motivation (1)	8	2,00	5,00	3,5000	,37796	1,06904
Self-confidence (2)	8	2,00	5,00	3,1250	,35038	,99103
Openness (2)	8	2,00	4,00	3,1250	,22658	,64087
Valid N (listwise)	8					

The numbers in Table 2 indicate the mean scores of qualities that autonomous learners need are ranged from 4.6 to 3.1 out of 5. Students' responsibility for learning is highest (4.6 out of 5), so it is concluded that students are responsible for their own learning and responsibility is among important personalities of autonomous learners. The second range can be seen in students' self-confidence (4.2 out of 5). Although they had to do many difficult tasks such as choosing the topic, searching for relevant sources, evaluating them and citing in their essays when writing an academic essay, they tried to complete their final product. Students' self-confidence was also examined in the challenge of writing tasks and students did not enjoy being set a challenge, so the mean scores for this quality is not high (3.1 out of 5). Another quality of an autonomous learner is motivation, and this quality is in the third range (4.0 out of 5). In other words, students tend to be motivated to work by assessment deadlines. In addition, students' motivation was investigated in their attitude toward finding information about new topics on their own, and the mean score for this attitude is 3.5 out of 5. Finally, students' independence of learning can be seen in their openness to new ways of doing familiar things and new learning experiences. The mean score for this quality 3.7 and 3.1 out of 5. That means students were not interested in new learning experiences because the mean score for this factor is lowest in the list. From these numbers, it can be concluded that by using the paper-based portfolio as a continuous assessment tool, the instructor could help students develop their independence of learning and this can be seen in some important qualities such as responsibility, self-confidence and motivation.

Table 3. Study habits of the paper-based group

	N	Minimum	Maximum	Mean		Std. Deviation
	Statistic	Statistic	Statistic	Statistic	Std. Error	Statistic
Meeting deadlines	8	4,00	5,00	4,5000	,18898	,53452
Attitude	8	2,00	4,00	3,3750	,26305	,74402
Planning	8	3,00	4,00	3,3750	,18298	,51755
Time Management	8	3,00	4,00	3,3750	,18298	,51755
Procrastination	8	1,00	1,00	1,0000	,00000	,00000
Valid N (listwise)	8					

The information in Table 3 reveals that students were very good at meeting deadlines when they studied independently. The mean score for this habit is 4.5 out of 5. The other three habits such as attitude toward lone working, planning, and time management have the same score (3.3 out of 5). Especially, the mean score for procrastination is 1 out 5. As explained above, if the mean score of this habit is low, the higher level of independence that students have. The mean score for this habit is 1 out of 5, so it can be inferred that these students occasionally found excuses for not getting down to work. As a result, though students' feeling happy, planning and managing their time for learning are at an acceptable range (3.3 out of 5), they were able to meet deadlines and were low in procrastination when working in dependently. It can be stated that when working with the paper-based portfolio, students could become very good at meeting deadlines, one of the important study habits of autonomous learners.

Table 4 demonstrates skills that students needed when they studied independently during their academic writing course. The mean scores are ranged from 4 to 3 out of 5. The highest mean score is for reflecting and the lowest score is for choosing learning strategies. From the numbers in this table, it can be concluded that students were very good at reflecting, a key stage in an experiential learning cycle including planning, action and learning. It means that being able to think critically about the experience, to identify the problems, to consider them in a new light in order to identify possible solutions for future learning. Other skills, though are not very high (ranged from 3.0 to 3.7 out of 5), are at acceptable levels.

In brief, for students in the paper-based group, basing on students' self-assessment after they completed the academic writing course, these students could gain three important qualities: responsibility, motivation, and self-confidence and reflecting, an important skill of an autonomous learner.

Table 4. Needed skills of the paper-based group

	N	Minimum	Maximum	Mean		Std. Deviation
	Statistic	Statistic	Statistic	Statistic	Std. Error	Statistic
Reflecting	8	3,00	5,00	4,0000	,18898	,53452
Collaborating	8	3,00	5,00	3,7500	,25000	,70711
Monitoring	8	2,00	4,00	3,5000	,26726	,75593
Self-assessing	8	2,00	4,00	3,3750	,26305	,74402
Selecting materials	8	3,00	4,00	3,2500	,16366	,46291
Reading	8	3,00	4,00	3,2500	,16366	,46291
Writing	8	3,00	4,00	3,1250	,12500	,35355
Planning	8	2,00	4,00	3,0000	,18898	,53452
Choosing learning strategies	8	2,00	4,00	3,0000	,18898	,53452
Valid N (listwise)	8					

Findings from the E-Portfolio Group

The mean scores for personal qualities of the E-portfolio group can be seen in Table 5. The scores are ranged from 4.2 to 3.3 out of 5. Like students in the paper- based group, those in the E-portfolio group highly appreciated their responsibility for learning experiences. The students in this group were also motivated to learn and gained enjoyment from their learning, and the mean score for motivation is 3.8 out of 5. This score is not very high, but it reveals that students were motivated enough to learn independently during their writing course. The third range falls on self-confidence (3.7 out of 5). That means even when writing tasks were difficult, they tried to stick with them. Also, the mean score for their enjoyment of being set a challenge is 3.3 out 5 (the lowest score in the list). Next to self-confidence is students' openness to new learning experiences and new ways of doing familiar things. The mean scores for this quality includes 3.6 and 3.5 out of 5.

Table 5. Autonomous learning of the E-portfolio group

	N	Minimum	Maximum	Mean		Std. Deviation
	Statistic	Statistic	Statistic	Statistic	Std. Error	Statistic
Responsibility	15	3,00	5,00	4,2667	,20625	,79881
Motivation (1)	15	3,00	5,00	3,8667	,21529	,83381
Motivation (2)	15	2,00	5,00	3,8000	,24300	,94112
Self-confidence (1)	15	3,00	5,00	3,7333	,18170	,70373
Openness (1)	15	2,00	5,00	3,6667	,23231	,89974
Openness (2)	15	3,00	4,00	3,5333	,13333	,51640
Self-confidence (2)	15	3,00	5,00	3,3333	,15936	,61721
Valid N (listwise)	15					

Besides the mean scores of personal qualities, those of study habits can be seen in Table 6. The information in this table indicates the mean scores of students' study habits are ranged from 4.3 to 1.3 out of 5. It is true that the students in the E-portfolio group were very good at meeting deadlines and the mean score for this study habit is 4.3 out of 5 (the highest score in this table). The second range can be seen in students' positive attitude toward studying independently, and the mean score of this habit is 3.8 out of 5. The third range can be found in students' time management for their independent learning and the mean score for this is 3.5 out of 5, or it can be stated that these students could manage their time for learning well. The number in Table 5 also indicates the mean score for students' ability to plan time for their learning after class is 3.2 out of 5. Although the score for this study habit is lower (in the fourth range) than that of the others, it reveals that students could plan their time for learning at an acceptable level. Finally, the

lowest score in the list of study habits can be seen in students'
procrastination, the mean score of which is 1.3 out of 5. From this score, it
can be inferred that students in the E-portfolio group sometimes found
excuses for not getting down to work.

Table 6. Study habits of the E-portfolio group

	N	Minimum	Maximum	Mean		Std. Deviation
	Statistic	Statistic	Statistic	Statistic	Std. Error	Statistic
Meeting deadlines	15	3,00	5,00	4,3333	,15936	,61721
Attitude	15	3,00	5,00	3,8000	,14475	,56061
Time Management	15	2,00	5,00	3,5333	,21529	,83381
Planning	15	2,00	5,00	3,2000	,24300	,94112
Procrastination	15	1,00	3,00	1,3333	,15936	,61721
Valid N (listwise)	15					

Table 7. Needed skills of the E-portfolio group

	N	Minimum	Maximum	Mean		Std. Deviation
	Statistic	Statistic	Statistic	Statistic	Std. Error	Statistic
Creating E-portfolio	15	3,00	5,00	3,8667	,21529	,83381
Collaborating	15	3,00	5,00	3,7333	,15327	,59362
Reflecting	15	3,00	5,00	3,6667	,15936	,61721
Monitoring	15	3,00	4,00	3,6000	,13093	,50709
Self-assessing	15	3,00	4,00	3,4667	,13333	,51640
Choosing learning strategies	15	3,00	5,00	3,4667	,16523	,63994
Planning	15	2,00	5,00	3,4000	,21381	,82808
Selecting materials	15	2,00	4,00	3,2667	,15327	,59362
Writing	15	2,00	4,00	3,1333	,13333	,51640
Reading	15	2,00	5,00	3,0667	,18170	,70373
Valid N (listwise)	15					

The numbers in Table 7 demonstrate the mean scores of 10 skills that
autonomous learners need. The scores are ranged from 3.8 to 3.0 out of 5. In
other words, though students did not highly evaluate their skills, it can be
seen that most of the skills are from 3.0 (OK) 3.8 out of 5 (or nearly success).
The highest mean score is for students 'ability to create E-portfolios, and the
lowest one is for reading skill (3.0 out of 5).

DISCUSSION

As presented above, the participants in both the paper-based portfolio and E-portfolio highly evaluated their responsibility for their autonomous learning activities after class. This quality can also be identified in one of their study habits (i.e., they are good at meeting deadlines). It can be concluded that by using the portfolio assessment, the instructor could train students to become responsible for their learning, and this finding is in line with the results of different previous authors such as Young (2008), Phan (2015), and Phan (2018). Also, the findings in Table 2 and Table 5 indicate that students in both groups were motivated to work independently after class though the mean score for this personal quality of the E-portfolio is partly lower than that of the paper-based portfolio group. Therefore, it can be stated that students could gain motivation when working with portfolios, and this is similar to the findings of Akçil and Arap (2009), Phan (2015) and Phan (2017). However, the numbers in Table 2 and Table 5 reveal that students in the E-portfolio group were less self-confident than those in the paper-based group; as a result, it can be proved that working with the E-portfolio negatively affected students' learning. This finding is different from Peréz Cavana (2012) because the participants of this author's study were very self-confident when they worked with E-portfolio. In spite of such a difference, this result is completely similar to the finding in different studies conducted by Phan (2015, 2017 and 2018); that means students were not self-confident enough when working on their E-portfolios.

The information in Table 3 and Table 6 shows that students in the E-portfolio group had a higher level of frequency of making excuses for not getting down to work than those in the paper-based group. When comparing the mean scores of skills of independent learners (Table 4 and Table 7), some differences between two groups can be seen. However, because these numbers were not statically analyzed and compared, the author has found it hard to know if these differences are significant or not. Thus, it is impossible to conclude that students in the paper-based group were better than those in the E-portfolio one at some skills they had to work on during their writing course.

Conclusion

From the analyzed and presented findings, it can be concluded that using the portfolio assessment in the academic writing class could help students to develop their responsibility and motivation. Some study habits, like meeting deadlines and feeling happy when working independently, may help them to become autonomous learners. Although these are positive indicators from the findings, the limitations of this study are inevitable. When carefully looking into the findings about autonomous learning, study habits, and skills, some differences between the paper-based and E-portfolio groups can be seen, so it can be clearly stated that the author did not critically and statistically contrast the findings from the two groups in order to know whether or not E-portfolios could be more effective than paper-based portfolios in helping students to learn independently after class because students' independence of learning is one of the core elements of the credit-based training system in all of the universitites in Vietnam. This is one of the most noticeable limitations of this study. Another limitation can be found in the findings comes from the responses of students' self-assessment of their autonomy, not from the instructor's assessment. If the author contrasted the results from students'self-assessment and the instructor's, there would be more interesting and persuasive evidence. The last limitation is that whether or not the portfolio assessment has helped students improve their writing skills was not examined.Therefore, some further studies on the portfolio assessment in writing classes should be conducted in the future. Future reseachers could employ different methods to collect data such as the instructor's observation and assessment of students' final products in their portfolios, and in-depth interviews with some participants if there is not significant correlation between their personal qualities and skills necessary for their independent learning.

REFERENCES

Akçil, U. and Arap, A. (2009). The opinions of education faculty students on learning processes involving E-portfolios. *Procedia Social and Behavioral Sciences 1,*395-400. Available at www.sciencedirect.com.

Aygün, S. and Aydin, S. (2016). The ue of E-portfolio in EFL writing: a review of literature. *ELT Research Journal*, 5, 3, 205-217.

Benson, P. (2006). Autonomy in language teaching and learning. In P. Benson; *Language Teaching*. 40, 1, 21-40. The United Kingdom: Cambridge University Press. Available at http://dx.doi.org/10.1017/S0261444806003958.

Barret, H. C. (2005). *White paper: Researching Electronic Portfolios and learner engagement*. Available at from http://electronicportfolios.org/reflect/whitepaper.pdf.

Brandes, G. and Boskic, N. (2008). E-portfolios: From description to analysis. *International Review of Research in Open and Distance Learning, 9(2), 1-17.*

Brown, H. D. (2004). *Language Assessment: Principles and Classroom Practices*. The United States: Longman.

Cakir, A. & Balcikanli, C. (2012). The Use of the EPOSTL to Foster Teacher Autonomy: ELT Student Teacher's and Teacher Trainers' View. *Australian Journal of Teacher Education*, 37, 3, 1-16. Available at: http://ro.ecu.edu.au/ajte/vol37/iss3/2.

Caner, M. (2010). Students' view on using portfolio assessment in EFL writing courses. *Anadolu University Journal of Social Sciences*, 10, 1, 223-236.

Chin, P., Reid, S., Wray, S. and Yamazaki, Y. (2015). *Academic Writing Skills*, Student's Book 3. Singapore: Cambridge University Press.

Douglas, H. (2012). E-portfolios as a strategy to support the development of self-directed learning skills. *Dissertation presented in part-fulfillment of the requirements of the degree of Master of Science in Information Technology in Education,* the University of Hong Kong. Available at hub.hku.hk/bib/B47469523.

Fahim, M. and Jalili (2013). The Impact of Writing Portfolio Assessment on Developing Editing Ability in Iranian EFL Learners. *Journal of Language Teaching and Research*, 4, 3, 496-503. Available at doi:10.4304/jltr.4.3.496-503.

Hung, S. T. A. (2012). A washback study on e-portfolio assessment in an English as a Foreign Language teacher preparation program. *Computer Assisted Language Learning*, 25, 1, 21-36.

Kabilan, M. K., and Khan, M. A. (2012). Assessing pre-service English language teachers' learning using E-portfolios: Benefits, challenges and competencies gained. *Computers & Education*, 58, 4, 007- 1020. Available at https://www.sciencedirect.com/science/article/pii/S0360 131511002922.

Kocoglu, Z. (2008). Turkish EFL student teachers' perceptions on the role of electronic portfolios in their professional development. *The Turkish Online Journal of Educational Technology*, vol.7, 3, n.p. Available at http://files.eric.ed.gov/fulltext/ED502674.pdf.

Lorenzo, G. and Ittelson, J. (2005). An Overview of E-Portfolios, *EDUCAUSE Learning Initiative*, edited by Diana Oblinger. Available at https://net.educause.edu/ir/library/pdf/ELI3001.pdf.

Macaskill, A. and Taylor, E. (2010). The development of a brief measure of Learner autonomy in university students. *Studies in higher education*, vol. 35, 3, 315-359. Available at http://shura.shu.ac.uk.

Moore, I. (2008). *What is learner autonomy?* Available at http://extra.shu.ac.uk/cpla/whatislearnerautonomy.html.

Nezakatgoo, B. (2011). The Effects of Portfolio Assessment on Writing of EFL Students. *English Language Teaching*, 4, 2, 231-241. Available at www.ccsenet.org/elt.

Nunan, D. (1997). Designing and adapting materials to encourage learner autonomy. In Benson and Voller (eds.), *Autonomy and Independence in Language Learning*, 192-203. The United Kingdom: Longman.

Obeiah, S. F. and Bataineh, R. F. (2016). The Effect of Portfolio-Based Assessment on Jordanian EFL Learners' Writing Performance. *Bellaterra Journal of Teaching and Learning Language and Literature*, 9, 1, 32-46.

Paulson, F. L., Paulson, P. R. & Meyer, C. A. (1991). "What Makes a Portfolio a Portfolio?" *Educational Leadership, 48,* 5, 60-63. Available at http://web.stanford.edu/dept/SUSE/projects/ireport/articles/eportfoli o.pdf.

Peréz Cavana, M. L. (2012). Autonomy and self-assessment of individual learning styles using the European Language Portfolio (ELP). *Journal of European Confederation of Language Centers in higher education* (CercleS), 1,1, 211-228. Available at: http://dx.doi.org/doi:10.1515/ cercles-2011-0015.

Phan, T. T. N., Tran, V.D.T. and Duong, Đ. H. T. (2014). Students' autonomy in the course of English Language Teaching Methods /Approaches (Part I) in the credit-based training system. *Journal of Science,* Ho Chi Minh City Open University, 36, 3, 108-121.

Phan, T. T. N. (2015). Student-teachers' self-assessment of their autonomy. *Journal of Science,* Ho Chi Minh City Open University, 14 (2), 70-82.

Phan, T. T. N., Le, P.T. and Doan, K. K. (2017). Using the E-portfolio on Google Sites to help student-teachers develop their autonomy in the credit-based training program. *Journal of Science,* Ho Chi Minh City Open University, 53 (2), 118-130.

Phan, T. T. N. (2018). The E-portfolios and Student- Teacher's Autonomy: Correlation Between their Willingness and Ability to Self-Study. *Proceeding of the International Open TESOL Conference,* in Ho Chi Minh City Open University (5-2018).

Reinders, H. and Balcikanli, C. (2011). Learning to foster autonomy: the roles of teacher Education materials. *Studies in Self-Access Learning Journal,* 2, 1,15-25. Available at http://www.sisaljournal/archive/mar 11/reinders_balcikalni.

Richards, J. C. and Renandya, W. C. (2002). *Methodology in Language Teaching: An Anthropology of Current Practice.* The United States: Cambridge University Press.

Schaefer, G. (2016). *Showcase your skills with an electronic teaching portfolio.* Available at http://www.learnnc.org/lp/pages/6437.

Smolyaninova, O. (2010). E-Portfolio for Teacher Assessment and Self-Evaluation. Available at *www.icl-conference.org/dl/proceedings/2010/ .../Contribution186.pdf.*

Spratt, M., Pulverness, A. and Williams, M. (2011). *The TKT Course: Modules 1, 2 and 3,* 2ⁿᵈ Ed.; The United Kingdom: Cambridge University Press.

Taki, S., and Heidari, M. (2011). The Effect of Using Portfolio-based Writing Assessment on Language Learning: The Case of Young Iranian EFL Learners. *English Language Teaching*, Vol. 4(3). Available at www.ccsenet.org/elt.

Thorbury, S. (2006) *An A-Z of ELT: A dictionary of terms and concepts in English Language Teaching.* Thailand: Macmillan Education.

Tosh, D., Light, T.P., Fleming, K. & Haywood, J. (2005). Engagement with Electronic Portfolios: Challenges from the Student Perspective. *Canadian Journal of Learning and Technology, 31,3.* Available at http://cjlt.csj.ualberta.ca/index.php/cjlt/article/view/97/91.

Uçar, S. and Yazaci, Y. (2016). The Impact of Portfolios on Enhancing Writing Skills in ESP Classes. *Procedia- Social and Behavioral Sciences* 232, 226-233. Available at www.sciencedirect.com.

Vangah, F.P., Jafarpour, M. and Mohammadi, M. (2016). Portfolio Assessment and Process Writing: Its Effect on EFL Students' L2 Writing. *Journal of Applied Linguistics and Language Research*, 3, 3, 224-246. Available at www.jallr.com.

William, L. (1997). Self-assess: why do we want it and what can it do? In Benson and Voller eds.), *Autonomy and Independence in Language Learning,* 79-91. The United Kingdom: Longman.

Wetzel, K. Strudler, N. (2006). Costs and Benefits of Electronic Portfolios in Teacher Education: Student Voices. *Journal of Computing in Teacher Education*, 22, 3, 99-108. Available at http://www.iste.org.

Wray, S. (2007). Electronic Portfolios in a Teacher Education Program. *E-learning,* 4, 1, 40-51. Available at doi: 10.2304/elea.2007.4.1.40.

Yastibas, A.E. and Cepik, S. (2014). Teachers' attitudes toward the use of e-portfolios in Speaking classes in English language teaching and learning. *Procedia - Social and Behavioral Sciences*. 176, 514-525. Available at www.sciencedirect.com.

Young, D. (2008). E-portfolio in Education: a cause for reflection. *Paper presented at SOLSTICE Conference 2008 at Edge Hill University.* Available at http://dera.ioe.ac.uk/13076/6/6213.pdf.

BIOGRAPHICAL SKETCH

Phan Thi Thu Nga

Affiliation: Ho Chi Minh City Open University

Education:
1995: Bachelor of Science in English Language Teaching (Can Tho University- Vietnam)
2003: Master of Science in Education (The University of Groningen – The Netherlands)

Research Projects

1. Research Project (2006) A survey on the autonomy of students at the faculty of foreign languages and solutions to help them to self-study effectively (a research coordinator)
2. Research Project (2008) The correlation between the scores of their placement test and the scores of school subjects during four academic years of 2003- intake students (a research coordinator)
3. Research Project (2009) A survey on the level on which student-teachers of English met the needs of the recruiters (a research coordinator)
4. Research Project (2012) A survey on English Language Teaching Methods at junior high schools in Ho Chi Minh City (the main researcher)

5. Research Project (2012) Time Management Methods for the sophomores of English in the credit-based training system (the supervisor of student researchers)
6. Research Project (2013) An investigation on the needs and awareness of English language learning of students in economic and technical majors at Ho Chi Minh City Open University (the supervisor of student researchers)
7. Research Project (2014) An investigation on how student-teachers of English study independently in the credit-based training system (the main researcher)
8. Research Project (2016) Using E-portfolios on Google Sites to help student-teachers of English to develop their autonomy in the English Testing and Assessment Methodology Course (the main researcher)
9. Research Project (2017) How to self-study for the English Teaching Knowledge Test (the supervisor of student researchers)

Published Articles

1. Phan T. T. N. (2003). The effect of the instructor's feedback strategies on the improvement of students' short essay writing skills. *Journal of Science*. Ho Chi Minh City Open University, 1 (6).
2. Phan T. T. N. (2015). Student-teachers' feedback after observing English classes in senior high schools. *Journal of Science. Ho Chi Minh City Open University*, 4 (43).
3. Phan T.T. N. (2015). Student-teachers' self-assessment of their autonomy. *Journal of Science. Ho Chi Minh City Open University*, 2 (14).
4. Phan, T. T. N. (2018). The E-portfolios and Student-Teacher's Autonomy: Correlation Between their Willingness and Ability to Self-Study. *Proceeding of the International Open TESOL Conference, in Ho Chi Minh City Open University* (5-2018).

Professional Appointments: Head of English Language Teaching Subdivision

EDITORS' CONTACT INFORMATION

Hoang Yen Phuong, Ph.D

School of Foreign Languages
Can Tho University
Can Tho City, Vietnam
E-mail: phyen@ctu.edu.vn

Thi Van Su Nguyen

School of Foreign Languages
Can Tho University
Can Tho City, Vietnam

INDEX

Second Language Acquisition: Methods, Perspectives and Challenges

EDITORS: Doris Luft Baker, Ph.D., Deni Lee Basaraba, Ph.D., and Cara Richards-Tutor

SERIES: Languages and Linguistics

BOOK DESCRIPTION: Collectively, this book provides the most up-to-date review of our current knowledge about how the complexities of each of the linguistic registers across mathematics, science and social studies extends far beyond content-area vocabulary and warranting an intentional, purposeful focus on language, particularly academic English during content-area instruction.

HARDCOVER ISBN: 978-1-53614-305-8
RETAIL PRICE: $230

The Linguistics of Vocabulary

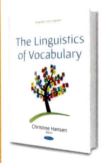

EDITOR: Christine Hansen

SERIES: Languages and Linguistics

BOOK DESCRIPTION: In this compilation, the authors open with an analysis of the formation of philosophical terminology in the history of Early-Modern Ukrainian culture; specifically, two philosophical concepts—dobro and blaho (добро and благо)—are the focus here.

SOFTCOVER ISBN: 978-1-53613-860-3
RETAIL PRICE: $82

THE LANGUAGE OF PEDAGOGY TODAY: WHAT ARE THE NEW TEACHING CHALLENGES?

AUTHORS: Rebecca Soler Costa and Turgay Han

SERIES: Languages and Linguistics

BOOK DESCRIPTION: In the field of pedagogy, there are different publications about the processes of didactic interaction in the classroom. The reader will find in this book a characterization of the language of pedagogy through the analysis of its neologisms, anglicisms and technicisms.

HARDCOVER ISBN: 978-1-53613-129-1
RETAIL PRICE: $160

TEACHING AND LEARNING ENGLISH FOR ACADEMIC PURPOSES: CURRENT RESEARCH AND PRACTICES

EDITORS: Lap Tuen Wong and Wai Lam Heidi Wong

SERIES: Languages and Linguistics

BOOK DESCRIPTION: Reviewing practices in different EAP classrooms can help readers reflect on the effectiveness of current classroom practices and teaching methodologies. The purpose of this book is to provide insightful information on current research and practices in EAP education across different contexts.

HARDCOVER ISBN: 978-1-53612-814-7
RETAIL PRICE: $230